The Songs of the Minnesinger,
Prince Wizlaw of Rügen

UNC | COLLEGE OF ARTS AND SCIENCES
Germanic and Slavic Languages and Literatures

From 1949 to 2004, UNC Press and the UNC Department of Germanic & Slavic Languages and Literatures published the UNC Studies in the Germanic Languages and Literatures series. Monographs, anthologies, and critical editions in the series covered an array of topics including medieval and modern literature, theater, linguistics, philology, onomastics, and the history of ideas. Through the generous support of the National Endowment for the Humanities and the Andrew W. Mellon Foundation, books in the series have been reissued in new paperback and open access digital editions. For a complete list of books visit www.uncpress.org.

The Songs of the Minnesinger, Prince Wizlaw of Rügen

With Modern Transcriptions of His Melodies and English Translations of His Verse

J.W. THOMAS AND BARBARA GARVEY SEAGRAVE

UNC Studies in the Germanic Languages and Literatures
Number 59

Copyright © 1967

This work is licensed under a Creative Commons CC BY-NC-ND license. To view a copy of the license, visit http://creativecommons.org/licenses.

Suggested citation: Thomas, J. W., and Barbara Garvey Seagrave. *The Songs of the Minnesinger, Prince Wizlaw of Rügen: With Modern Transcriptions of His Melodies and English Translations of His Verse.* Chapel Hill: University of North Carolina Press, 1967. DOI: https://doi.org/10.5149/9781469658360_Thomas

Library of Congress Cataloging-in-Publication Data
Names: Thomas, J.W. and Seagrave, Barbara Garvey.
Title: The songs of the minnesinger, Prince Wizlaw of Rügen : With modern transcriptions of his melodies and English translations of his verse / by J.W. Thomas and Barbara Garvey Seagrave.
Other titles: University of North Carolina Studies in the Germanic Languages and Literatures ; no. 59.
Description: Chapel Hill : University of North Carolina Press, [1967] Series: University of North Carolina Studies in the Germanic Languages and Literatures. | Includes bibliographical references.
Identifiers: LCCN 68064588 | ISBN 978-1-4696-5835-3 (pbk: alk. paper) | ISBN 978-1-4696-5836-0 (ebook)
Subjects: Wizlaw III, prince of Rügen, -1325. | Minnesang. | Minnesang — History and criticism. | German poetry — Middle High German, 1050-1500. | German poetry — Middle High German, 1050-1500 — Translations into English.
Classification: LCC PD25 .N6 NO. 59 | DCC 781/ .96

"The Songs of the Minnesingers" by Barbara Seagrave and J.W. Thomas was originally published in the *Journal of English and Germanic Philology,* and material from that work is reprinted here with permission of the present copyright holder, University of Illinois Press.

ACKNOWLEDGMENT

During the preparation of this volume we have become indebted to a number of individuals and institutions to which we would like to express our appreciation. For their assistance in supplying photographic reproductions of manuscripts and rare books we are grateful to the libraries of the following universities: The Free University of Berlin, The Eastman School of Music, Göttingen, Hamburg, Jena, Leipzig, and Tübingen. Librarians to whom we are particularly indebted are Mrs. Harold Hantz, of the University of Arkansas, and Dr. Annemarie Hille, of the University of Jena – the former for her constant search for rare books which we needed to examine, the latter for supplying us with free photostatic copies of the Wizlaw Manuscript and with valuable information concerning an as yet unfinished doctoral dissertation. For permission to use material from our *Songs of the Minnesingers*, 1966, we are indebted to the University of Illinois Press. For their assistance in preparing and proof-reading the manuscript we are grateful to Professor and Mrs. Bruce Benward, the former of the Music Department of the University of Wisconsin, and to Mrs. Mark Doyle. Finally, we should like to thank Dean Adkisson and the Graduate Council of the University of Arkansas for a generous research grant.

CONTENTS

CHAPTER I	The Life of Prince Wizlaw of Rügen	1
CHAPTER II	The Minnesinger Tradition	34
CHAPTER III	The *Sprüche*	49
CHAPTER IV	The Minnesongs	59
CHAPTER V	The Melodies	71
CHAPTER VI	The Manuscript	85
CHAPTER VII	The Texts	98
BIBLIOGRAPHY		149
INDEX OF FIRST LINES		153
INDEX OF NAMES		154

CHAPTER ONE

THE LIFE OF PRINCE WIZLAW OF RÜGEN

Wizlaw III was born about the year 1265 as the first son and heir apparent of Prince Wizlaw II and his wife, Agnes of Braunschweig-Lüneburg. The principality over which the infant's father reigned was approximately the size of the state of Rhode Island and consisted of the Baltic island of Rügen and the nearby coastal area of North Germany extending southward to the Peene River. The island, with its high chalk cliffs rising out of the sea, its rugged hills and dark forests, and its almost countless large and small peninsulas and bays, is one of the most picturesque regions of Germany. The adjacent mainland, a little more than a mile distant, is a low plain, which in Wizlaw's time was heavily forested, but now consists largely of green fields and meadows, dotted with small villages.

The principality of Rügen was a part of that area which had been abandoned by its Germanic inhabitants during the early centuries of the Christian era and had been subsequently settled by the Slavic Ranen tribes. It remained Slavic until after 1168 when it was forcibly Christianized by King Waldemar I of Denmark with the aid of Pomeranian and Mecklenburgian allies. From that time on Germanic people returned to this land of their remote ancestors in ever-increasing numbers, so that by the time of Wizlaw III the Slavic population was in the minority and the Slavic language was disappearing. Strangely enough, the immigrants did not come from Denmark, which had established a nominal sovereignty over the principality, but from the German lands to the south and southwest. They came as priests, monks, artisans and tradesmen, bringing with them their language and culture.

Wizlaw III was a direct descendent of the first Christian ruler of the principality, Jaromar I, who in turn, according to a sixteenth century chronicle by Thomas Kantzow (p. 4), was descended from the pagan princes who had ruled Rügen for more than a century previous to its Christianization. At any rate, the family was a very old one, from which had sprung the ruling houses of most of the small countries of the Southern Baltic region, the majority of which shared a common emblem, that of a griffin and a lion. Wizlaw's ancestors had been vigorous and astute rulers in times when only the brave and the wise could survive. For the history of Northern Germany during the century before his birth had been one of frequent wars and rapidly changing alliances, against the constant background of a struggle between the two greater powers, Denmark and Brandenburg, for the domination and assimilation of the smaller lands. The converted pagan, Jaromar I, had adapted himself readily to this situation by allying himself with Denmark as a protection against Brandenburg and his immediate neighbors, Pomerania, East Pomerania and Mecklenburg, and by courting the favor of the powerful Church as a protection against Denmark. This policy was generally followed by his successors and with such success that by the time of Wizlaw III the principality had grown considerably through the addition of territories on the mainland. The minnesinger's grandfather, however, Jaromar II, had been obliged to choose between his two chief allies and, at the instigation of Pope Alexander IV, carried out two highly successful campaigns against Denmark. He conquered many Danish castles and cities, including Copenhagen, and, had it not been for the intervention of Norway and Sweden, might have placed his son-in-law, Duke Erich of Schleswig, on the Danish throne.

With the death of Jaromar II the minnesinger's father, Wizlaw II, became the ruling prince of Rügen. Less of a warrior and more of a statesman than Jaromar II had been, his son abandoned the hostilities against Denmark and devoted himself to protecting and extending the boundaries of his country by peaceful means. With a view to insuring himself against aggression from Brandenburg he established friendly relations with the neighboring states of Pomerania, Mecklenburg, Cammin, and Schwerin and with the semi-autonomous cities along the southern Baltic coast. He also concerned himself more than his predecessors had done with domestic problems, particularly those of the cities which were springing up in the mainland area of his country. In order to stimulate its commerce and attract immigrants to it, Wizlaw II gave additional land to Stralsund, the largest of his cities, and granted its citizens special privileges, including exemption from military draft and free jurisdiction over its internal affairs. Similar, but more restricted privileges were given to the inhabitants of the smaller cities, Barth, Tribsees and Loitz. As a result of these and other internal reforms the economy of the country was greatly improved and it soon recovered from the financial distress brought about by the wars of Jaromar II. This increased prosperity enabled Wizlaw II further to cement the cordial relations which had always existed between his country and the Church by lavish donations to churches and monasteries, not only in Rügen, but also in the neighboring lands of Holstein, Mecklenburg, and Pomerania, and even as far away as Braunschweig, Denmark, and Norway.

One of the most effective means of territorial aggrandizement in those days of hereditary monarchies and indistinct national borders was marriage. Marriages, as Wizlaw II well understood, were not only more effective than formal alliances, but also brought in new territories in the form of doweries and even offered the possibility that an entire land might eventually be annexed through inheritance rights. His own marriage and those of his children were, therefore, carefully arranged with respect to political and territorial advantage. His marriage to Agnes of Braunschweig-Lüneburg not only established a politically valuable relationship with an influential ruling family, but also put the court of Rügen in contact with the more refined culture of middle and southern Germany, a connection which the practical monarch may not have fully appreciated, but which was of great importance to his children. The court life of Braunschweig was that of a cultivated society which valued good manners, splendid social functions, music, verse, and even learning. Agnes herself had been a student in the monastery school at Quedlinburg and was probably quite well educated for her time. She brought with her to Rügen something of the courtly life and values to which she was accustomed.

Since our knowledge of Wizlaw II and his family is drawn almost exclusively from state documents, we can only surmise as to their private life. The ancestral castle of the princes of Rügen was the Rugard castle which was built by Jaromar I about 1170 on a lofty elevation in the northeastern part of the island of Rügen. However, by the time of Wizlaw II Rugard was rather far removed from the centers of population of the principality and was somewhat inaccessible. He and his family, therefore, resided chiefly at the castle of Hertesburg on the forested peninsula of Darss, occasionally visiting other castles in the mainland towns of Barth, Prohn, Tribsees and Loitz. They apparently did not have a residence in Stralsund and probably stayed at one of its two monasteries while in the city. There were eight children: Wizlaw and Sambor, who followed their father as rulers of Rügen; Jaromar, who became ruler of the ecclesiastical state of Cammin; Euphemia, who married King Hakon V of Norway; Margarete, who became the wife of Duke Bogislaw IV of Pomerania; Helena, who first married Johann of Mecklenburg and later Bernhard II of Anhalt-Bernburg; a fourth daughter, of whom only the name, Sophie, is known and a fourth son, who probably died in childhood, since not even his name appears in extant records.

There is reason to believe that the minnesinger, Wizlaw the Younger, as he was called to distinguish him from his father, attended during his youth a secular school in Stralsund which was presided over by a Magister Ungelarde (*Verfasserlexikon*, IV, 634), a scholar, musician, and poet, who may have been brought from Braunschweig by Agnes when she came to Rügen. Through him the young Wizlaw not only became well versed in the songs of the South German minnesingers, but also mastered the fundamentals of musical and poetic composition. Such instruction as a part of a young prince's education, though unusual in the north, was quite in keeping with the chivalric ideal of much of Hohenstaufen Germany. His further education would have taken place at Hertesburg Castle where he and his brothers learned to ride and use sword and lance and mastered the niceties of court etiquette. For recreation there was good hunting in the forests and sailing on the open sea or in the narrow bay between the peninsula and the mainland.

We know little of the joys, but something of the sorrows of Wizlaw's youth. One of his earliest memories would have been of the death in 1270 of his grandmother, Euphemia, the wife of Jaromar II, and her burial in the Monastery of Johannis, in Stralsund, which her warlike husband had helped to found. Another early memory would have been of the death in 1272 of his aunt Margarete and her husband, Erich I of Schleswig, whom Jaromar II had tried in vain to place upon the Danish throne. The death of the nameless brother could also be added to the early sorrows. However, Wizlaw's light-hearted minnesongs give no hint of a blighted youth and one can assume that his boyhood was in general a happy one. He liked to travel and at least by his later teens was permitted to accompany his father on the latter's frequent journeys to Lübeck, Rostock, Prenzlau and other cities in the neighboring countries. And it may well be that he accompanied his father on the latter's crusade against the heathen of Livonia. Wizlaw II, incidentally was perhaps less interested in spreading Christianity by this crusade than in establishing his brother, Jaromar, as a ruler over a part of Prussia, an attempt which, had it been successful, would have served the dual purpose of extending his own influence and restricting the growing power of the Teutonic Knights in that area. However, the death of Jaromar in the same year brought an end to the plan.

Immediately after the Livonian Crusade the poet's father reluctantly became involved in two wars simultaneously. The first was between Brandenburg and the Southern Baltic countries, including Rügen; the second was between Norway and England on one side and a league of German cities on the other. The principality of Rügen neither gained nor lost territory as a result of the hostilities.

After the death of Jaromar, who had served as Wizlaw II's chief advisor and as regent during his longer absences from the country, the monarch came to rely more and more upon the minnesinger and the latter's younger brother, Sambor, for assistance in the government and from 1283 the name of the former appears frequently in documents together with that of his father (Fabr., IV, Abt. 4, 117). However, the cooperation between father and sons must have been somewhat difficult in such unsettled times, for, according to tradition, both Wizlaw the Younger and Sambor had inherited much more of the warlike disposition of their grandfather than of the judicious nature of their father. A second brother of Wizlaw the Younger, Jaromar, was destined for the Church and is mentioned in a document of 1280 as being a 'scholaris' in Stralsund. Later he became priest of the Nikolai Church in the same city and in 1289 was elected head of the Bishopric of Cammin, a state on the Baltic coast east of Rügen. Although he died before being formally ordained as bishop, Jaromar's brief reign was very successful. Aided no doubt by the advice of his politically astute father, he was able to utilize the rivalry between Pomerania and Brandenburg in such a way as to win complete secular independence for his country. With his death in 1294 Wizlaw II again saw his ambitions for his family unexpectedly and tragically frustrated.

In the same year, 1289, in which Wizlaw's brother, Jaromar, became the ruler of Cammin, his sister, Helena, married Johann of Mecklenburg. This alliance between the reigning families of the two adjoining countries promised to be of great importance to their mutual security and represented a diplomatic success on the part of Wizlaw II equal to that of Jaromar's election. The wedding must have been a really gala occasion, for Detmar, the Lübeck chronicler, writing almost a century later, not only records the event, but even gives the exact date on which it took place and praises the virtue and beauty of the bride (I, 164). It must have been an occasion such that even the heir apparent would not have hesitated to turn entertainer, and it is quite probable that Wizlaw performed with some of his merry songs.

At Hertesburg Castle there were probably many gay festivals with feasting, dancing and singing, for it seems to have been a favorite stopping place with the travelling minstrels of the day. And the center of revelry was the eldest son of the host, young Wizlaw, who sang and played with the minstrels and commanded the admiration of all of the guests. Two of the singers who visited and entertained at the Rügen court were der Goldener and Frauenlob (*Verfasserlexikon*, II, 57 and I, 644-658) both of whom composed songs in praise of their noble colleague. Der Goldener was a talented, but obscure North German poet, only five of whose songs are extant. In addition to the song about Wizlaw, he composed verses about Wizlaw's neighbor, Margrave Otto the Long, of Brandenburg. Frauenlob, also known as Heinrich of Meissen, was much better known and much more prolific than was der Goldener, for, in addition to three long *Leiche* and thirteen minnesongs, there are 448 stanzas of *Sprüche* extant which have been attributed to him. Frauenlob performed at one time or another at most of the larger courts in the German-speaking lands and composed songs in honor of many of the prominent rulers of his day. He is buried at the cathedral at Mainz, although the exact location of the grave is not known.

A prose translation of der Goldener's song in praise of Wizlaw (von der Hagen, III, 52) is as follows:

> In the Garden of Honor a garland was woven that was so splendid and elegant that it was fitting for a prince who was loyal, manly, wise, and of high nobility. Thus would he need be who should place it on his head. Faithfulness, purity, and innocence have carefully braided the wreath; generosity and moderation have illuminated it with gleaming splendor. Then I asked knights and ladies, who was virtuous enough to wear it. They spoke, 'We can say without reservation who deserves to wear it: Wizlaw, the young hero of Rügen.'

Frauenlob's praise was even more unrestrained than was that of der Goldener (von der Hagen, III, 123). In his typically flowery language he sang:

> Reach out, my heart, and help my thoughts forge a song of praise which would be most suitable to all members of the art. He, to whom I give this praise, would rather have it, I believe, than an ex-

cellent beverage, since a glass of clear wine does not taste as good to him as praise from the mouth of a poet. When he sees anywhere rude customs, shame colors his cheek as with dragon's blood. He has an angel's courage for good works. He strengthens himself with virtue so greatly that none can see the lack of it in him. Therefore shall the wandering minstrels sing his praises far and wide. His blossoming fame admonishes me to make known to the people the name of him whose praise is sent into these lands. It is, for this I pledge my word, Wizlaw, the young hero of Rügen.

Even when one considers that it was not unusual for minstrels to compose songs as these in honor of their hosts and patrons, one feels that such extravagant praise must have been evoked by an especially interesting and attractive personality.

Other facets of Wizlaw's character not mentioned by the two poets – rashness and haughtiness – are revealed by an event of about the year 1290 which Detmar relates (I, 176). He tells of how Wizlaw made a pilgrimage to the Christian church which had been established at Riga, in Livonia, and to which his father had given certain estates in Rügen. While in the city he was accosted by a merchant, probably a German, who asked him to pay a debt which he had contracted. When Wizlaw responded angrily to the request, the merchant became so enraged that he drew a knife and stabbed the young nobleman in the leg. The effect of the wound was such that the latter limped from that time on. This incident had prophetic implications. Not only did it reveal something of Wizlaw's disdainful attitude toward the merchant class, but also shows the increasing independence of the merchants with regard to nobility. It is not surprising that Wizlaw after he became ruler of Rügen should have had so many difficulties with the merchants of his own city of Stralsund.

Metaphorically speaking, he was to receive many such wounds under similar circumstances.

Not long after Wizlaw returned from Riga, his father became involved in the affairs of two of the nearby states and with unfortunate consequences. When Heinrich I of the tiny country of Werle died, his neighbor, Nikolaus II of Parchim drove the former's sons from their homeland and annexed it. The principality of Rügen, probably at the insistence of the adventurous Wizlaw and Sambor, intervened on behalf of the sons, while the Bishop of Schwerin supported Nikolaus. In the hostilities that followed Wizlaw II and several hundred of his knights, including perhaps his sons, were captured and for a short time imprisoned in Parchim. In order to gain freedom for himself and his knights the prince had to accept the sovereignty of the bishop over the territory of Tribsees, although the former continued to hold it as a fief.

The struggle over the Werle succession was followed by a longer and more destructive war, the cause of which was the death in 1294 of the childless Mestwin II of East Pomerania. Here again one is tempted to see the impulsive hand of Wizlaw in the diplomacy of his aging father. The latter, with characteristic forethought and sagacity, had begun as early as 1277 to plan for the eventuality that Mestwin might die without direct heirs. In that year he had ceded a small piece of outlying territory, which he had inherited from his mother, to Brandenburg in an attempt to establish a cordial atmosphere for future negotiations concerning East Pomerania. These negotiations took place in 1289 and provided for a division of the country between Rügen and Brandenburg in the event that Mestwin should have no sons. Such an arrangement would not only enlarge their boundaries, but also block the threatened expansion of the territory of the Teutonic Knights. When Mestwin died, however, the margraves of Brandenburg renounced their agreement with Rügen. This poor faith on their part may have been caused by greed, the hope of annexing all of East Pomerania. But it may have been the result of a personal affront to one of the margraves of Brandenburg. Probably with the encouragement of the government of Rügen, Nikolaus the Child, of Mecklenburg-Rostock, broke his engagement to Margarete, daughter of Margrave Albert of Brandenburg, in order to marry Wizlaw's niece, the daughter of Duke Bogislaw IV of Pomerania. The cementing of a Rügen-Mecklenburg-Pomerania alliance at the expense of Brandenburg offered definite advantages to the former countries, but also entailed certain risks, particularly with regard to the partition of East Pomerania. One can only think that, regardless of how their father may have assessed the situation, Wizlaw and Sambor were as willing to enter a winner-take-all struggle as were the margraves of Brandenburg. The results of the bloody war, which lasted from 1295 to 1302, was that neither the allies nor Brandenburg reaped any fruits of victory. For, weakened by the long struggle, the combatants were unable to offer much resistance when other nations intervened. Poland and Bohemia were, therefore, able to occupy East Pomerania while Norway and Denmark were successful in re-establishing the latter's sovereignty over Mecklenburg.

Whether or not it was the rash ambition of Wizlaw which provoked the war, it was certainly the statesmanship of his father that brought it to a conclusion which, if not successful, was at least not disastrous. For when he married Wizlaw's sister, Euphemia, to King Hakon V of Norway, a realignment of forces took place that left Rügen intact when peace finally came.

This marriage was as important to Norway as it was to Rügen, although not in the same way. Euphemia was apparently very much like Wizlaw. She was an educated and strong-willed woman who, as queen of Norway, exerted a definite influence on the culture of the land and sometimes even on its politics. Like Wizlaw she was enamored with the ideas of chivalry and introduced a punctilious etiquette into the Norwegian court as well as extravagant dress and splendid festivities. More important, however, is the fact that she commissioned translations of German and French chivalric romances into Norwegian and encouraged the writing of similar works by Danish poets. It was primarily Euphemia who introduced Norway and Norwegian literature to chivalry.

With the conclusion of hostilities the old Wizlaw II was probably glad to escape from his impoverished country and the increasing tension between his headstrong sons by a prolonged stay at the court of his son-in-law in Norway. He died there in 1302 and was buried in the Church of St. Mary in the city of Christiania, leaving considerable property to Norwegian churches and his principality to Wizlaw, now Wizlaw III, and Sambor. The brothers apparently soon realized that a joint administration was impossible and, therefore, decided upon a division of property and responsibility, which, however, did not include a political partition of Rügen. Such a plan might have enabled them to live in peace had they been left alone, but they were not. Some of the nobles and especially the abbot of the monastery at Neuencamp, now Franzburg, sought to promote their own interests by turning the two princes against each other. We know nothing of whatever actual conflict may have taken place between Wizlaw and his brother, but the agreement, of May 1, 1304, by which it was settled is still extant (Fabr. IV, Abt. 1, 33). In it they promised to help each other against any enemy and to refrain from attempting to rob each other of subjects, cities or castles. The effectiveness of the agreement was probably never tested, for in the same year Sambor died without heirs and Wizlaw became sole ruler of Rügen.

At the time of Sambor's death Wizlaw was about thirty-nine, still single and, in so far as scanty evidence permits one to judge, still very youthful in spirit. He liked to travel about, both within Rügen and abroad, and to entertain as lavishly as his finances would permit. Although he probably did little composing any more, he enjoyed music and literature and the company of musicians and scholars. And one can assume that he sometimes entertained his guests with his gay and occasionally risqué songs. He has been described as a knightly gentleman, a politician of dubious talents and an even worse financier (Kuntze, p. 25). One can imagine him as a sort of Don Quixote who played the role of a hero of Arthurian romance, as a knight in armor who glorified combat and chivalry. At any rate, he was not the man to rebuild and unify a war-torn and divided country or to understand and come to terms with the new force which was already weakening the medieval feudal system, the cities.

One of Wizlaw's first acts after becoming ruler of all of Rügen was to renew the fealty oath to Denmark. The titular sovereignty of Denmark over Rügen had existed in theory since the time of the Christianization of the latter country, although the princes of Rügen had always conducted their affairs quite independently of Denmark. That Wizlaw should choose to acknowledge formally Danish sovereignty probably stemmed from his love of tradition and ceremony rather than necessity, for it is quite likely that he could have safely refused to renew the oath. After all, King Hakon of Norway was his brother-in-law and the Danish king, Erich Menved, was not then in a position to anger his neighbor to the north. At any rate Wizlaw and the chief members of his court journeyed to the Danish castle of Vordingbord on the island of Seeland where he was entertained with the elaborate festivities which he loved. There he vowed loyalty to Denmark and received in fief the island of Rügen, the land of Sund, the lands of Tibusees, Grimme and Barth: 'videlicit terram ruje, Terram sundis, Terram grimmis, Terram Tribuses, et Terram barth cum ciuitatibus, muncionibus, rominibus, et ceteris earundem pertinenciis...' (Fabr. IV, Abt. 1, 37). That Wizlaw, for all his romantic tendencies, had something of his father's shrewdness is indicated by the fact that the Danish king, no doubt at his vassals's insistence, specifically renounced any claims he might have had to properties left by Sambor.

It must have been very soon after Wizlaw's journey to Seeland that he married, for his first wife, Margarete, is first mentioned in the year 1305 (Fabr. IV, Abt. 1, 39). However, neither the date of the marriage nor the family from which the bride came can be definitely ascertained. There were pressing reasons of state for Wizlaw to marry at this time. Not only was he the last of the male members of the family in the direct line of succession, but also his recent fealty oath to King Erich raised the possibility that Rügen might be incorporated into Denmark if Wizlaw should die without an heir. This danger apparently concerned the prince much less than it did his subjects. Indeed, it was Wizlaw's pro-Danish policy as much as anything else which gradually alienated both the minor nobility of Rügen and the influential citizens of Stralsund. However much Wizlaw may have enjoyed his bachelorhood, his subjects were concerned and most certainly took steps to terminate it.

Unfortunately for the political stability of the country, however, the marriage of Wizlaw and Margarete remained childless, a fact which encouraged King Erich to take further steps to strengthen his position in Rügen. His first move was to conclude agreements with the families of Gristow and Putbus, two collateral lines, whereby they were to receive the peninsulas of Wittow and Jasmund respectively in the event that Wizlaw should die without a son (Fabr. IV, Abt. 1, 61). In exchange for these properties they were to renounce all claim to the throne. The following year (1310) Erich persuaded Wizlaw in a meeting held at Ribnitz, in Mecklenburg, to declare him to be the heir in the event that Wizlaw's line should die out. This eventuality seemed probable at the time, for Wizlaw's wife apparently had died prior to the meeting at Ribnitz, and Wizlaw was already about forty-five years of age. The question of succession became less urgent, however, when he married Agnes, a daughter of Count Ulrich of Lindow, and had a son and a daughter. The date of the marriage is not known, but it must have taken place in or near the year 1310, perhaps soon after the succession agreement between Wizlaw and King Erich.

It may have been at the time of his second marriage that Wizlaw built a new castle close to the town of Barth on the mainland, which became his chief residence for the remainder of his life. It is probable that his mother, who outlived Wizlaw II, continued to reside at the Hertesburg Castle. The castle at Barth was much less isolated than was either Rugard or Hertesburg, indeed, it was on the main coastal route which linked the North German cities and was, therefore, well located for the active social life which Wizlaw enjoyed. It soon became a convenient and popular stopping place for the wandering singers and scholars who passed through the country.

Aside from the matter of isolation, there may have been another reason for Wizlaw to establish his chief residence on the mainland rather than on the island of Rügen. Whereas the inhabitants of the mainland were chiefly Germans, the islanders were for the most part of Slavic blood. Indeed a Slavic dialect continued to be spoken by a few of the inhabitants until the end of the 14th century, and like most isolated ethnic and linguistic groups they were very conservative with regard to social and cultural innovations. The minnesinger, however, like his father was oriented toward the German culture of the South and quite possibly could not even speak the language of his ancestors. At any rate there appears to have been a marked lack of sympathy between the islanders and their ruler throughout the latter's reign.

During the years following his second marriage Wizlaw had little opportunity for social activities, for he and his country were caught up in a confusion of wars which rocked the

Baltic coast for six years. Not only did the struggle between Denmark and Brandenburg for the domination of North Germany reach its peak during this time, but also civil wars broke out in the Southern Baltic states as a result of the attempts of the rulers to curb the growing power and independence of the cities within their realms. These internal struggles furthered the designs of King Erich, for he realized that the cities were as strongly opposed to his plans as was Brandenburg and were equally dangerous as opponents. Wizlaw, whether because of an exaggerated sense of loyalty to his titular sovereign or because of personal friendship, supported King Erich fully and shared his defeat.

During the thirteenth century the rulers of the Southern Baltic countries had stimulated the growth of their cities by granting them special political, legal and economic privileges, and had in many ways encouraged their growth from small fishing villages to large and prosperous commercial centers. However, by the beginning of the fourteenth century the princes had begun to realize that within the borders of their lands existed political and economic units which were practically autonomous and had powerful navies and armies to defend themselves, not only from foreign aggressors, but also from their own sovereigns. This internal danger to the latter's authority was increased when the cities of Wismar and Rostock in Mecklenburg, Greifswald in Pomerania, and Stralsund in Rügen joined the free city of Lübeck in the years 1293 and 1296 in formal pacts which dealt not only with matters of trade, but also with mutual defense. There is no doubt but that Wizlaw, with his traditional ideas on the relationship of lord and vassal, was exceedingly irritated by being obliged to deal with his own city, Stralsund, as with a foreign power. He had reason also to be jealous of it, for, although Stralsund could field a formidable army and possessed a large navy, it was not obliged to lend him a single soldier or ship. Its citizens were for the most part subject only to the laws of the city, even when beyond its boundaries, and its flourishing import-export trade was tax exempt. This last privilege of the city must have been particularly galling to Wizlaw, for while he was always short of money, the city enjoyed ever-increasing prosperity. The new city hall was both larger and more luxurious than any of his castles; the Stralsund Church of St Nicholas, built in 1311, was the most stately in the land and, as a crowning insult, there was always plenty of money for new walls and fortifications. Nor were the individual citizens inclined to be modest about their wealth. Indeed, the city council felt it necessary to restrict private festivities by city ordinances. One, of the year 1310, restricts the number of guests which could be invited to a wedding celebration to 120 and the number of professional entertainers to 6. These celebrations usually lasted for several days. When one considers the independence and the wealth of the city it is not surprising that the envious monarch once referred to Stralsund as an inflamed abscess on his country.

Wizlaw's resentment against the presumption of the citizens of Stralsund was naturally shared by his courtiers, as is seen in the following incident which was recorded by an anonymous chronicler (Fabr. IV, Abt. 2, 49). The two mayors and some of the prominent citizens of Stralsund were guests of Wizlaw on the island of Zingst, not far from Hertesburg Castle. A deer was killed and, while the servants were cutting up the animal, one of the noblemen called to them, saying that they should save as much meat as they could, for otherwise only the boors and fat bourgeois, 'rustici et smerscnidere,' of Stralsund would get any of it. Such remarks were hardly calculated to establish congenial relations between city and court. However, many of the noblemen, particularly those having estates on the island of Rügen, were well disposed toward the leading citizens of Stralsund and sometimes joined them in opposing the will of the prince. Some of the nobles shared the dislike of the citizens of Stralsund for

Wizlaw's pro-Danish policies, but there were apparently others who simply believed that the best way to protect their own privileges was to defend those of Stralsund and to weaken the power of the prince.

King Erich's first step in his plan to reestablish Denmark's authority in North Germany was to capitalize on the resentment of the rulers against the wealth and power of the cities and thus win allies for the subjugation of the latter. Even before he had begun to act two incidents occurred which greatly favored his plans. The first concerned Lübeck, the largest and strongest of the cities. Lübeck had for some time been threatened by Count Gerhard of Plön, the stepfather of King Erich, together with a large number of princes and knights from the area which is now Schleswig-Holstein. Instead of turning to the league of cities or to the German emperor for assistance the citizens of Lübeck placed themselves under the protection of the Danish king for a period of ten years. By this act the city and its wide-spread trading interests, to be sure, were saved from attacks by Count Gerhard, but the alliance of cities was appreciably weakened. Lübeck did not leave the league, but when the representatives of the cities met in Rostock in 1310 the Lübeck delegation declared that they would not take part in any action against Denmark.

The second incident took place in 1311 and concerned another of the cities, Wismar. Prince Heinrich of Mecklenburg wished to celebrate the marriage of his daughter in his city of Wismar and, therefore, requested its citizens to make provisions for accomodating him, his retinue, and guests inside of the city walls during the time of the festivities. One cannot know as to whether the prince had ulterior motives, but, at any rate, the city council had no intention of opening the gates to a large number of armed knights and refused their sovereign's request. The marriage had to take place elsewhere and the angry prince used the occasion to enlist the aid of the assembled guests, one of whom no doubt was Wizlaw, in a military action against the city. Wismar, however, was not only strongly fortified, but its navy was quite capable of keeping open its outlet to the sea so that it could withstand a long siege. Prince Heinrich and his friends, therefore, were obliged to ask assistance from King Erich and his navy. This was the opportunity for which the Danish king had been waiting, but he had too much respect for the strength of the league of cities to be hurried into any precipitate action. He devised a scheme which would win him the largest possible number of allies and would divorce the cities from any potential outside support.

The greatest festival ever to take place in North Germany in medieval times was arranged, with invitations going out to the kings, princes, dukes, and counts of all of Central and Northern Europe. The occasion was the knighting by King Erich of Waldemar I of Brandenburg and, since Brandenburg was the traditional opponent of Danish expansion, was ingeniously calculated to neutralize, if not actually win over, the most probable ally of the league. The celebration was to be held in the city of Rostock, which since the year 1300 had been a vassal city of Denmark. In choosing one of the league cities as the meeting place, Erich once more displayed his cunning. Rostock was presented with the choice of admitting him and his knights or of insulting its king and half of the rulers of Europe. The citizens, of course, recognized their dilemma, but found a middle course. They refused to admit the entire host of visitors into the city, but gave permission for Erich, Margrave Waldemar, and a specifically limited number of their followers to enter. This compromise was naturally disappointing to the Danish king, but he agreed to it and had a pavillion erected in the middle of the city where he could receive Waldemar. During the night before the guests arrived, however, an irresponsible mob of citizens tore down the structure and Erich to his considerable satisfaction, for it furthered his plans, was forced to move his court outside of the city and entertain his guests there.

It was a splendid occasion, comparable only to the festival which Emperor Friedrich Barbarossa had held more than a century earlier in Mainz and which purportedly had been attended by fifty thousand knights. In front of the walls of Rostock sprang up another city, a great expanse of gaily colored tents which surrounded a broad parade ground where thousands of knights with pennants and plumes daily participated in the manifold activities of a medieval tournament. Nor did the celebrating pause at nightfall. Then, by the lights of a sea of torches, whole oxen were consumed and wine barrels emptied while the guests were regaled by the wandering entertainers who had gathered there from all of the neighbouring lands: dancers, acrobats, jugglers, small theatrical groups which performed amusing and often coarse skits, musicians and singers. It was an immense spectacle that was praised by chroniclers and poets for years afterwards. The renowned Frauenlob was there and immortalized the occasion in one of his compositions (von der Hagen, III, 126). 'The knighthood which was assembled before Rostock,' he sang, 'far excels in splendor all else that is known to me.' A later poet, writing in the Kirchberg Rhyme Chronicle of the Year 1378, went into more detail (Kuntze, pp. 13-14):

> On the same occasion many a nobleman was knighted, there was a great deal of jousting and all sorts of knightly contests. There was beautiful singing by the poets and the sweet sound of strings. There was courtly revelry, tilting and knightly swordplay. There was excellent food; they served game meat and tame. There were wells in the earth and whoever was thirsty helped himself to beer or wine, generously as if it were water. The horses were fed in a lavish fashion – everything was done

extravagantly: a great mountain of oats was piled there and everyone carried it away as if it were sand.

Detmar (I, 196-7) also gives an account of the occasion.

One can imagine the delight of the romantic and gregarious Prince Wizlaw with all of the pageantry and congenial company. He himself probably performed before small groups of his peers, of whom there were many. Among those known or thought to have been present were the counts of Holstein, the princes of Mecklenburg, the dukes of Pomerania, the princes of Anhalt, the dukes of Lüneburg, the dukes of Saxony, nobility from Thuringia, Poland, Silesia and, of course, from Denmark, Rügen and Brandenburg, all with their retinues of knights. Many church dignitaries were also there, including the archbishops of Lund, Magdeburg and Bremen.

Behind the festivities of the Rostock tournament of 1311 the true business of the meeting went forward according to plan. King Erich reminded his guests of the insult which he and also they had received from the citizens of Rostock, Heinrich of Mecklenburg told of his recent difficulties with his city of Wismar, and Wizlaw complained bitterly of the arrogance of his subjects in the city of Stralsund. The assembled princes formed a loose alliance and made preparations for hostilities against the league of cities. Even before the festival was over Heinrich sent a delegation to Wismar to renounce them formally as subjects and soon afterwards began an attack on the city with the aid of his new allies. A blockade was established and an attack by land was begun. The other cities immediately sent ships to break the blockade of Wismar and were successful, but the land siege continued and the citizens found it advisable to negotiate while their walls were still intact. Since Heinrich did not know how long he could keep his allies with him, he, too, was not opposed to negotiations and the outcome, though definitely a defeat for

Wismar, was not a complete surrender. The citizens reaffirmed their allegiance to Prince Heinrich and accepted sharp restrictions on their military commitments to the other cities of the league. With this defeat the strength of the league as such was broken for a time.

Meanwhile the princes also attacked Rostock, not only with the goal of subjugating it, but also to limit the assistance which this city could give to Wismar. For a time the Rostock fleet and army kept the enemy at bay and carried out destructive raids along their coasts, including that of Denmark, which at first was not participating directly in the war. Having been attacked, however, King Erich brought a large army to Rostock and joined Duke Erich of Saxony, Margrave Waldemar of Brandenburg, and the others in the siege. The city could not resist such a large force; it lost its outlying defenses to the enemy, was cut off from outside help, and had to sue for peace. The provisions of the treaty were harsher than those imposed upon Wismar. Heavy reparations were assessed and the city was obliged to agree never to enter into any alliance which was directed against Denmark.

It was now the turn of Wizlaw and his recalcitrant city of Stralsund. His position, however, was not very favorable for a number of reasons. King Erich had been forced to return home to put down a revolt in his own land, many of the allies which had been won at the Rostock festival had tired of the war and returned home, and others, especially Waldemar and the dukes of Pomerania, were showing signs of a change of heart with regard to King Erich's campaign against the cities. Wizlaw nevertheless made preparations to attack Stralsund, but the city, somewhat shaken by the fate of Wismar and Rostock, at once offered to negotiate. The settlement, which involved a modest sum to be paid by Stralsund as an indemnity and a guarantee by Wizlaw of the city's traditional privileges (Fabr. IV, Abt. 2, 24), did not satisfy the prince at all, but the forces at his disposal were not strong enough for him to make greater demands at that time. Unfortunately the humbling of his city had become a point of honor with him, an obsession which in the years that followed was to alienate him completely from many of the lesser nobles of Rügen as well as from the citizens of Stralsund.

Wizlaw's next move was to reestablish a part of the alliance which had broken up, and to this end he concluded military pacts with Mecklenburg, Holstein, and Saxony. It was then a matter of waiting for a favorable opportunity to exert further pressure on the city. The opportunity came rather unexpectedly when the dominant party in Stralsund lost its influence in the city council and a more democratic city government came to power. This was headed by Johann and Godeke of Güstrow, uncle and nephew, members of a rich patrician family with which Wizlaw had long been on cordial terms. The latter at once moved into the Neuencamp Monastery, which was just outside of the city, and from there sent secret messengers to negotiate with his friends. Since they needed his help to maintain their new position in the city, the Güstrows agreed to Wizlaw's terms for Stralsund and urged the city council to accept them. Aware of the prince's new alliances, the council understood the implied threat in Wizlaw's overtures and accepted the conditions immediately. These were most favorable to the prince and represented far greater concessions than those which had been won from Wismar and Rostock. He regained the right, which had been given up by his father, to collect certain tariffs, he could restrict the special legal privileges of the citizens, and he obtained assurances that the city would enter into no foreign commitments without the permission of its sovereign. Even this considerable success, however, did not satisfy Wizlaw and he was seeking further concessions when the political situation in the city again changed; his friends on the council were driven out of the city, his sovereignty was repudiated, and an alliance was formed with Brandenburg. This was a bitter disappointment for Wizlaw who had believed himself so close to his goal. Unable to make a frontal assault unassisted on the strong fortifications of the city, he destroyed those properties of the citizens of Stralsund which were outside of the walls and the properties of many of their supporters. In return the citizens constructed forts at various places on the mainland and even on the island of Rügen, from which they raided the farms and villages of the prince.

The indications are that Waldemar of Brandenburg was not unfavorably disposed toward Wizlaw, but he was determined to check a further expansion of Danish influence and he knew that the subjugation of Stralsund and the resulting collapse of the league could only further Danish ambitions. Therefore, together with Duke Wartislaw of Pomerania, he crossed over the Peene River and seized Wizlaw's castle and estate at Loitz before the latter had an opportunity to assemble his allies. These were discouraged by the sudden entrance of Brandenburg and Pomerania into the conflict, and internal difficulties as well as a war with Sweden prevented King Erich from coming to Wizlaw's assistance. The prince would have been in a desperate situation had not the problems which arose at the death of the German Emperor Heinrich VIII forced Waldemar to turn his attention elsewhere. As it was, the further hostilities between Wizlaw and Stralsund were confined to raids on Stralsund shipping by the former and raids on coastal villages by the latter until, in the closing days of the year 1314, a peace was arranged. Through its provisions Wizlaw was obliged to pay a thousand pounds of silver to Waldemar in order to regain Loitz, and Stralsund was once more placed under the sovereignty of Rügen with, however, all of its traditional rights restored.

Wizlaw, to be sure, did not give up his intention of subduing his city; indeed he could hardly afford to, for he had mortgaged much of his property as well as his future tax income to finance the campaign against Stralsund and he needed revenue from its flourishing trade to pay off his debts. He immediately began to form new alliances. To assure himself of the friendship of the Danish king he accepted Loitz, which till then had been his exclusive property, from Erich as a fief. He also concluded a military pact with the rulers of Werle and obtained a pledge from the prince of Anhalt whereby the latter was to come to his aid, if needed, with one hundred mounted troops. In addition Wizlaw did all that he could to build up his own forces, mortgaging such property as was not already pledged. Stralsund also was not idle, but the only allies it could hope for, aside from Brandenburg, were within the country of Rügen. Here, however, it had considerable success. The heads of the families of Gristow and Putbus, who had entered into the succession agreement with Denmark, declared themselves openly to be on the side of Stralsund and promised to accept no new prince without the concurrence of Stralsund in the event that Wizlaw's line should die out (Fabr. IV, Abt. 2, 35). This declaration was, of course, a bid for the support of the city for their claims to succeed Wizlaw. Two other powerful noblemen of the island of Rügen, Heinrich and Borchert of Osten, joined them in promising to defend Stralsund, and other knights no doubt made secret commitments. Although the knights on the mainland were for the most part loyal to their prince, Wizlaw's position in the country at large was becoming daily more insecure. The struggle which he had begun at Rostock with the enthusiasm of a crusader for a cause, the divine right of kings, had become a desperate and weary struggle for survival.

Although there continued to be minor skirmishes between Wizlaw's forces and those of Stralsund, they did not lead at this time to a full-scale war. Wizlaw's nephew, Wartislaw IV of Pomerania, could see what his uncle could not, that a general war might benefit Denmark or Brandenburg, but could only be harmful to the other countries of the north. He, therefore, prevailed upon both parties to sign another treaty, the Brudersdorfer Peace Treaty of 1315, in which the terms of the preceding pact were confirmed and in which Wizlaw agreed to take no action against Stralsund for at least three years. It is probable that this treaty, unlike that of 1314, was signed in good faith, for Stralsund's trade had suffered considerably by the recurring strife and Wizlaw's resources were exhausted. He could borrow no more money on his own assets, but was reduced to seeking co-signers for his loans. Had it not been for Denmark, the prince of Rügen would now probably have turned his attention to rebuilding his land and to the cultural and intellectual pursuits in which he was still deeply interested.

In the meantime the inexhaustible King Erich had patched up his quarrel with Sweden and was eager to make another attempt to expand his influence in North Germany. This time he recognized his chief opponent as Waldemar of Brandenburg and laid his plans accordingly. A great alliance was formed which included almost all of the states of North Germany, the Scandinavian countries of Jutland, Norway and Sweden, and even Poland, whose ruler, Duke Wladislaw, particularly desired to see his neighbor, Brandenburg, defeated. The declared goal of the new alliance was to complete the work of the Rostock alliance, that is, to defeat Stralsund, and thus the unfortunate principality of Rügen became the battlefield of the greater powers. Wizlaw once more undertook the difficult task of raising an army to support the alliance. Although he had recently signed a nonaggression pact with Stralsund, he really had no choice but to join one side or the other, for a position of neutrality without doubt would have cost him lands and indemnities from the victors, whoever they might be. Never before had troops been so hard to get. At the first indication of a renewal of hostilities twelve of the most prominent knights and 125 squires of the island of Rügen, speaking for the population of the entire country, declared their independence of Wizlaw and signed a defense pact with

Stralsund (Fabr. IV, Abt. 3, 30). Although the mainland area remained for the most part loyal to the prince, his credit was seriously impaired by this open defection. Since he had hardly any money and little else to mortgage, he was reduced to the point of pledging his own person as security. A document of that time reveals that he promised to deliver himself as a prisoner to the towns of Grimmen or Tribusees, should he not pay the knights and squires enlisted there (Fabr. IV, Abt. 3, 29).

In the end Wizlaw did assemble a respectable number of troops. Some joined him out of loyalty or friendship, some because they disliked the citizens of Stralsund, others because they wished to restrict the growing influence of Brandenburg, and a few perhaps who thought that Wizlaw would somehow be able to pay them for their aid. The events which followed are succinctly described by Detmar (I, 206):

> After Easter then the king of Denmark took council with his advisors and with all the help which he could get in Denmark and in German lands. He bade them all come before Stralsund; they were all willing to do this as soon as the tidings came to them. Saxony, Holstein, the Slavs and others of his helpers all hastened to come there. Duke Erich of Saxony came there with the first ones and encamped by the city very close to Hainholz. Then the citizens quickly sent their messengers for help: it came in the same night. In the morning early they sallied forth with their guests to where they knew the enemy to be. They captured the duke and slew a great part of his best men; the prisoners they brought into the city. The king then besieged the city by water; he of Rügen, their lord, he of Mecklenburg and many other lords, they besieged them by land. When they long had tried all man-

ner of battle strategems against the citizens and had won little gain thereby and also see that the citizens well defended their city and their honor, then they went away from there, each his own way. Duke Erich was then consigned to his brother-in-law, Duke Wertislaw, whose sister he had recently taken; that one then had to further consign him to the margrave. Therefore he remained a prisoner very nigh to three years; then he was freed for eight thousand fullweight marks of silver, which his land paid with great loss.

Other fourteenth century documents provide information concerning the campaign which is not contained in the Detmar account and Kantzow (pp. 84-85) also presents an account of the battle. According to them Duke Erich of Saxony-Lauenburg entered Rügen in June of 1316 at the head of an army of about 5,000 men, which was large for those times. Wizlaw and his troops joined Erich and both proceeded to Stralsund and encamped near the city to wait for their allies and intercept any troops which might try to join the citizens of Stralsund. However, advance contingents of Brandenburgers and Pomeranians were already within the city walls and the defenders decided to launch an offensive before the main body of their enemies should arrive. The surprise attack, as Detmar reports, was very successful. Erich and many of his men were captured and Wizlaw, according to rumor, was barely able to escape by sea. However, the campaign was by no means over, for King Erich of Denmark and the other allies soon arrived to support the remnants of the Saxon and Rügen armies. In order to forestall participation by Prince Heinrich of Mecklenburg, Waldemar invaded that country from Brandenburg and there discovered why Heinrich was called 'the Lion,' for the margrave was severely wounded in the battle which ensued and barely escaped capture. However, despite this defeat the

Brandenburg forces were still powerful enough to play an important role in the subsequent hostilities. Stralsund was besieged by land and sea for many months, but was able to hold out until dissension among its enemies and exhaustion on the part of both enemies and friends brought the hostilities to an end. The chief combatants, Denmark, Mecklenburg, and Brandenburg concluded a treaty in 1317 which affected Rügen only by ratifying the *status quo ante bellum*. The preliminaries were agreed upon the preceding December and the peace treaty was signed in May at Sulz in Mecklenburg. Most of the North German states were represented. Among those present were King Erich, Margrave Waldemar, the princes of Mecklenburg, the dukes of Stettin and Lüneburg, probably also Duke Rudolf of Saxony, two counts of Holstein, and many other Danish and German knights. Wizlaw was also there and witnessed the final collapse of his plans to subjugate Stralsund.

Forsaken by his allies, rejected by many of his own knights and impoverished to the point that he had to sell many of his estates and at least one village, Wizlaw, with what grace he could summon, did what had to be done. In June of 1317 he appeared in the city hall of Stralsund and there confirmed all of the traditional privileges of the city and renounced all of the claims which he had previously made against it. He also gave up the rural lands which he had seized from the citizens. They returned to him his castle at Prohn and the village of Parow which they had occupied. Wizlaw then made his peace with the knights of the island of Rügen and began the rebuilding of the country. To gain funds for this task Wizlaw pledged the nation's tariffs to the city for a time and agreed to stamp coins only in the city. Other privileges which the city obtained, perhaps for a price, included the right to supervise its schools (Fabr. IV, Abt. 3, 56-59). Historical records give no indication of any further unpleasantness between Wizlaw and Stralsund, indeed; it is quite probable that the citizens of the city increasingly gave him their support in unifying Rügen and improving its economy.

More important for the peace of Rügen than the rapprochement between Stralsund and its prince were the foreign events which transpired two years later. For just as the civil war in the country was largely the result of a power struggle which involved all of northern Germany, so too was peace in Rügen made possible by a cessation of that struggle. In the year 1319 both Waldemar of Brandenburg and Erich of Denmark died, leaving behind successors who were too weak to carry on the rivalry which had existed between their countries for well over a century. In the same year Wizlaw's brother-in-law, King Hakon of Norway, also died, which further served to loosen the former's ties with Scandinavia and Scandinavian politics. To be sure, Wizlaw once more journeyed to the castle of Vordingbord to renew the fealty oath to Denmark, but this time it was no more than a formality. The prince had long disliked Erich's brother and successor, Christoph, and refused to extend the succession agreement by which Denmark should inherit Rügen if Wizlaw were to die without a male heir. Instead, in 1321, he made a similar pact with his sister Margarete's son, Duke Wartislaw IV of neighboring Pomerania. This change in succession rights no doubt did as much as anything else to improve relations between Wizlaw and his anti-Danish subjects.

The headings on the various documents which Wizlaw signed during his later years reveal that he was still travelling a great deal, partly no doubt for reasons of state, partly also because of a nervous energy that would not let him rest, partly because of a love of society and adventure. His favorite residence was still the castle at Barth, but he sometimes stayed at Loitz in the far south of his land, and, especially in summer, at Hertesburg Castle on the lonely peninsula of Darss where he could look out on the broad sea to the north and hunt with friends in the deep forest which enclosed the castle on the other three sides. Wizlaw seldom visited the island of Rügen. It may well be that his strict sense of feudal honor could forgive disloyalty in a city merchant, but not in a nobleman. At any rate, his relations with the knights of the island apparently remained rather cool. It is no doubt indicative of Wizlaw's feeling toward all of these knights that he failed to make any mention of the succession claims of his relatives of the houses of Putbus and Gristow in the pact with Duke Wartislaw.

Although the main facts of Wizlaw's public life are known, there are almost no documents extant which reveal anything of his private life. One manuscript, a provision list kept by his steward, however, does tell of some of his activities during four summer weeks of his later life in which he and his family together with a large retinue resided mainly at Hertesburg Castle (Fabr. IV, Abt. 4, 88-91). Wizlaw was visited there by two scholars who were perhaps also poets, Master Johannes of Kamp from the city of Rostock and Master Petrus from Denmark. Duke Erich of Saxony, Wizlaw's comrade-in-arms during the crushing defeat at Stralsund, came to see him, bringing many courtiers and friends. A Count of Wittenberg also visited Hertesburg Castle, perhaps to hunt deer with Wizlaw in the forest of Darss or on the neighboring island of Zingst. Wizlaw was absent twice during the four weeks. He spent a few days at his castle in Loitz and visited his nephew, Duke Wartislaw, in the city of Wolgast. If the period covered by the manuscript is at all typical, and it seems to be, Wizlaw's interest in scholarly and literary matters and his enjoyment of society were as strong in his last years as in his youth. The steward's list indicates that the prince entertained on a rather large scale – the purchase of 900 plates was quite in keeping with the expenditures for food during the month.

The last two important occasions of record in Wizlaw's life were the marriage of his daughter Agnes and the engagement of his son Jaromar. Agnes was married in September of 1324 in the castle at Barth to Count Albrecht II of Anhalt, a nephew of Wizlaw's antagonist in the Stralsund campaign, Waldemar of Brandenburg. Through this marriage the prince of Rügen wished to establish friendly relations with Brandenburg and also, no doubt, to show to all that he would no longer be used as a pawn for Danish imperialism. The engagement of his son in the following year (1325) came about as a result of certain serious disagreements which had arisen between Heinrich of Mecklenburg and Wartislaw, in which Wizlaw, as the latter's uncle, had become involved. With dearly bought wisdom Wizlaw invited Heinrich and his retinue to come to Barth to discuss an amicable solution to the difficulty. The meeting was so successful that an engagement was arranged between Jaromar and Heinrich's daughter Beatrix, even though both were still in their early teens (Fabr. IV, Abt. 4, 86). This engagement was a master stroke of diplomacy in that it not only smoothed over past unpleasantnesses, but also secured for Jaromar a strong protector when he should succeed his father.

With peace and prosperity in his land and his succession ensured, Wizlaw, who was about sixty, but still vigorous, could now look forward to a quiet old age of travel and literary pursuits. However, the misfortune which had followed him all of his life struck again with the sudden death of Jaromar, only two months after his engagement. His father, broken by the tragic destruction of hopes and plans, died November 8 of the same year in Barth Castle and was buried in the Monastery of Franzburg (Detmar I, 220). Thus ended the line which ruled Rügen in pagan and Christian times throughout its entire history as a state. After Wizlaw's death his nephew, Wartislaw IV of Pomerania became ruler of Rügen, but did not unite the two countries. Wartislaw died only eight months after Wizlaw and Rügen was seized by Prince Heinrich of Mecklenburg. Stralsund and the Pomeranian city of Greifswald, however, took the part of Wartislaw's widow and after two years of war drove Prince Heinrich out of the country. Rügen was then formally incorporated into Pomerania and disappeared as a separate political unit.

Although our knowledge of Wizlaw's character and personal life is quite limited, by reading between the lines of the chronicles and records one forms a picture of a very personable man who enjoyed society and festivities immensely, who loved music and literature, and may have been something of a gay Lothario. At the same time he possessed a great deal of nervous energy and had a tendency toward explosions of anger and rash action. He was also an impractical idealist who sometimes behaved as a knight in Arthurian legends. Certainly his fatal loyalty to King Erich and his almost suicidal attempts to subdue Stralsund can best be explained by an outmoded chivalric concept of the relation of lord to vassal. In short, he was a poet and musician whose chief and perhaps only qualification for ruling was a keen awareness that the blood in his veins was that of centuries of high nobility.

CHAPTER TWO

THE MINNESINGER TRADITION

The musical and poetic compositions of Wizlaw, Prince of Rügen, make up an Indian Summer of an art tradition which was at its height some one hundred years before he began to write. This tradition was a product of the courtly culture of the Hohenstaufen period (1138-1254) and was the most characteristic expression of German chivalry. Chivalry was an all-embracing creed that governed the knight's varied activity and in which he was as carefully indoctrinated as was the priest in his theology. At about age seven the young nobleman was sent away to another court to receive his education: if the father were influential, the boy might even be accepted at the court of the emperor. There, while serving as a page, he was taught to ride and use a sword and lance and was introduced to the rules of the court. At age fourteen or fifteen the youth became a squire, whose duty it was to attend the knight in battle or in tournaments, to care for his horse and weapons, and to act as his aid. When the squire reached his early twenties and was sufficiently versed in military skills and the meticulous etiquette of the court, he was dubbed knight. But chivalry was more than a military and social code. Its chief goal was the achieving of a perfect balance between temporal and spiritual good, the combining of the enjoyment of earthly pleasures with the service of God. The ideal of the knight was a spiritual-physical harmony, a seriousness tempered with gaiety, a nobility joined to beauty. He strove for a union of the diverse elements of his heritage: the Germanic virtues of loyalty and bravery, the humanity and compassion of Christianity, and the Greek and Oriental delight in beauty, grace, form, and pageantry. This complete harmony finds its best expression in the mystic symbol of the holy grail which Wolfram's hero seeks in the courtly epic *Parzival*. It is also expressed in the glorification of *minne*, a highly formalized concept of love.

An exact definition of *minne* is not possible, for not only did the hundred or more minnesingers who used the term frequently disagree as to its meaning, but there is also sometimes little consistency in its employment in the individual songs of the same composer. The general conception of *minne* is that of an erotic passion which is both physical and spiritual, but which reaches no fulfillment. Although the concept did not appear in the earliest minnesongs, but was introduced later from Provence and France, it received almost immediate acceptance in Germany, for it filled a literary and aesthetic need. *Minne* is on the one hand a secularization of the adoration of the Virgin Mary, in that the knight fixes his affections on a highborn lady who, like the Virgin, must be worshipped from afar. On the other hand it is a refinement and sublimation of the drives and virtues of ancient pagan times. The chief virtues of the Germanic heroes were *stæte* and *triuwe*. Where the Germanic hero showed his constancy (*stæte*) by enduring untold hardships in difficult campaigns and his loyalty (*triuwe*) by dying in battle to defend and support his leader, the medieval knight could demonstrate the same characteristics, and less painfully, in a social situation. The minnesinger speaks not only for himself, but for all knights when he sings of the pains of love. He emphasizes his ability (and theirs) to endure suffering by portraying his passion and frustration as limitless. He demonstrates his (and their) unswerving loyalty by insisting that, although the lady does not in the least reward his affection, he will remain faithful to her forever. The lady in the minnesong usually is not portrayed as an individual, but is sketched only in the broadest terms, her chief characteristics being haughtiness, beauty, and desirability. However, the song is actually less about her than about *minne* itself and is less a praise of *minne* than an exaltation of self, a demonstration of nobility in suffering. The beauty of the lady and the passion of the knight are both so great that, in spite of his high regard for virtue, he tries to seduce her. But the virtue of the lady is so unassailable that she is able to resist him in spite of her own great passion and the ardent persuasion of the knight. This is the situation which is central to most of the songs, although the goal of the knight is usually veiled by polite ambiguities. It is a game that reveals the balance of body and spirit which was the chivalric ideal.

There is a general assumption, which is not definitely confirmed by either the lyric or the narrative literature of the Hohenstaufen period, that the heroine of the minnesong was a married lady. The advantages of choosing the wife of another as the object of the minnesong are obvious. Her position offers a sufficient reason for the lack of success of the lover's suit; it can add a spice of naughtiness to the song; and it enables the minnesinger to pretend that the object of his affections is among his listeners, the female portion of which consisted almost exclusively of married women. However, the fact that the object of the lover's desires is married is never expressly stated, nor is it really necessary to the song to assume that she is so. She, and with her all ladies of the court, is raised to an ideal of perfection of charm and beauty for which one longs intensely and unceasingly and, since no great ideal is ever attained in actuality, it is logically and aesthetically inevitable that she cannot be won.

According to the cult of *minne* it was the duty of the knight to serve his lady in every way, but in actuality this service consisted in singing her praises and declaring his devotion. However, she had to remain anonymous. No name, family, residence, or specific characteristics could be mentioned. Her identity had to remain a secret because of the jealous rivals, of the spies who would destroy the reputations of the lady and her lover, of the guardians whose duty it was to keep them apart. These were the enemies of lovers who had to be outwitted. They were indistinct, nebulous figures who were no more than symbols of the difficulties which stand in the way of true love; they are literary conventions which can be traced back to Ovid.

Although the minnesong of the early Hohenstaufen period was in general a song of longing and unsatisfied desire, there was a type of minnesong, the *tagelied* or dawn song, in which love finds consummation. However, the emphasis was rarely on the joys of love, but rather on the sorrows of parting. For the night of love has passed when the song begins and the ardent lover must now tear himself away from the weeping lady before their tryst is discovered. Once more nobility of character is demonstrated by depth of pain and sadness.

The peculiar concept of love which the word *minne* indicates and the terminology and ritual which accompanied it were of Romance origin and first appeared in German song as a result of the influence of Provençal troubadours and French trouvères in the latter part of the twelfth century. The earliest of the German minnesingers portrayed love as a quite natural and simple emotion, and were as likely to sing of the joys as of the sorrows of love. This type of love song occasionally reappeared after the beginning of the thirteenth century in the later works of Walther von der Vogelweide, the works of Neidhart von Reuenthal, and in some of the works of their successors. However, these later songs which lacked the formalized concepts of *minne*, though composed in a sophisticated style and for a courtly audience, had as their heroines peasant girls rather than ladies of the court. Among knights and ladies the cult of *minne* was observed – at least as a tradition and literary pretense – by even the last of the minnesingers. One may seek the origins of this Venus worship in either classical and oriental culture or in the Christian tradition. Actually, one finds in the cult of *minne* both pagan-physical and Christian-spiritual elements, existing in a harmonious unity. *Minne* was the essence of beauty, of nobility, of devotion; and in the service of *minne* the courtly society could demonstrate all of the subtle manners, aesthetic sensibility, and controlled emotion of their sophisticated culture.

The compositions of the minnesingers can be grouped into three categories: the minnesong, the *Spruch*, and the *Leich*. The earliest extant minnesongs consist of a single stanza of two rhymed couplets. Each line has six accented syllables, a varying number of unaccented syllables, and is divided in the middle by a caesura. Appearing at almost the same time, however, is a somewhat more complicated form in which the single stanza has a tripartite structure. There is an *Aufgesang* (rising song), made up of two *Stollen*, and an *Abgesang* (falling song). The two *Stollen*, which are metrically and musically identical, consist usually of three or four lines each in which the scene or situation is described. The *Abgesang*, which is usually longer than a single *Stollen* but not as long as the entire *Aufgesang*, describes the resolution of the situation. The lines are either long with a caesura or short. The rhyme scheme of the early minnesong shows couplets or alternating rhyme.

The musical form most commonly used for the tripartite minnesong is known as the *Barform* and is similar to the Romance *ballade* (A A || B). In the *Barform* the same melody is used for the two *Stollen* and a new melody is used for the *Abgesang*. A literal repeat of the entire *Stollen* melody at the end of the *Abgesang* (A A || B A) produces the most common form of the late minnesong and is the favorite pattern of the meistersingers who followed and imitated the minnesingers.

The Romance influence, which began to affect the minnesong about the year 1175, produced an increasing complexity of form, introducing lines of varying length and intricate rhyme patterns. The minnesongs began to be polystrophic with each stanza having the same structure and melody. However, the individual stanzas might or might not consist of *Aufgesang* and *Abgesang*. The themes of the songs also became more varied. Based on content, the most common types of minnesongs are: ladies' songs, alternating songs, salutations, dawn songs, and crusade songs. The lady's song appears chiefly and almost exclusively in the earliest period of the minnesong. It is a monologue by a woman in which she bewails the absence or neglect of her lover. The alternating song presents a dialogue between two lovers. Sometimes they are in each other's presence, sometimes they convey their words by means of a messenger. The alternating song is often combined with a dawn song. The salutation is a greeting by a knight in which he praises his sweetheart and declares to her his love. The crusade song sometimes, but not always, contains a love motif and describes the sorrows of parting as well as a solemn dedication to a religious duty. Several of the crusade songs were composed to be sung in chorus by the crusaders.

The *Spruch* is a song, usually in one stanza, that treats subjects other than love. Its structure does not differ basically from that of the minnesong. The three most common topics which the *Spruch* presents are matters of a didactic or religious nature, the personal experiences of the singer, and political situations and events. The didactic *Sprüche* may relate moral stories or proverbs, discuss virtues and vices, or treat the relationship of man to God. Of greater importance to the history of the minnesingers are the *Sprüche* which deal with their personal experiences, for it is from them that we have, in the case of most of the minnesingers, our only knowledge concerning their lives, residences, and positions. Indeed, we would not even know the names of some of the minnesingers if it were not for such *Sprüche*. The authorship of Wizlaw's songs, for example, would not be known, had he not mentioned his name in several of his compositions. The political *Sprüche* also frequently help to supply biographical data concerning their authors, since the matters which they discuss enable one to establish approximate dates for their composition. Although many of the knights composed *Sprüche*, they were more popular with bourgeois composers who, for their part, were generally less interested than the knights in the minnesong. Therefore the relative number of *Sprüche* increased rapidly during the thirteenth and fourteenth centuries as the proportion of bourgeois composers increased.

The longest lyric form used by the minnesingers was the *Leich*, derived from the Romance *lai*. It has a variable structure related both to the Latin sequence and to dances grouped in a series of parts like the *estampie*. It consists of a large number of stanzas whose construction varies in meter, rhyme scheme, line length and stanza length. In musical structure, the stanzas often repeat the same music, frequently with different endings to the same tune. The poetic material of the *Leich* includes both religious and secular themes. Those with secular content were often composed as an accompaniment for dancing, with the varying forms of the stanzas indicating different types of dances.

The melody of the minnesong, *Spruch*, or *Leich* together with its specific metrical structure makes up its *Ton*, although the term is sometimes used to indicate the metrical structure alone. The minnesingers were very proud of the different number of *Töne* which they could devise, and they produced a great variety. Walther von der Vogelweide composed about one hundred melodies and metrical patterns, and other minnesingers were nearly as inventive. To use someone else's *Ton* was highly unethical and caused the offender to be branded as a *Ton* thief. Indeed the minnesingers rarely used the same *Ton* for two of their own minnesongs; however, they had no qualms about using one *Ton* for several *Sprüche*. The general tendency throughout the history of the minnesong was toward increased complexity of *Ton* to the extent that many of the later songs are little more than pretentious displays of metrical virtuosity. This development was almost inevitable when one considers the importance of originality of form. The emphasis on originality was not so great with respect to musical composition as it was with metrical structure and the practice of fitting new texts to pre-existent tunes was rather widespread. Indeed, one of Wizlaw's texts, that of Minnesong II, may have been set to the melody of another. However, even with music the minnesingers seem to have been a little sensitive about borrowing, for they were much more inclined to use a Latin, Provençal or French melody for one of their songs than a melody by another minnesinger.

During the early years of the thirteenth century while the minnesong was still in full bloom, there appeared a type of song, the courtly village song, which was composed to accompany dancing. And it was about the same time that the first *Leiche* were composed which can readily be identified as *Tanzleiche* (dance lays). These forms, particularly the former, became very popular and continued to be written throughout the subsequent history of the minnesong. It should not be assumed, however, that the courtly village songs and the dance lays were the first songs of the court which accompanied dancing. Indeed, it may be that many of the early minnesongs were sung during dances. This is especially likely in the case of songs which treat the seasons of the year, for dancing and singing were essential elements of the traditional folk festivals in which the different seasons were celebrated. The songs which mention dancing make a distinction between the slow and measured *hovetanz* (courtly dance) and the lively village dances, which were also popular at the courts.

The oldest of the village dances were the *reien*, choral dances performed in a line or circle and using both gliding and leaping movements. The singing was led by the *vorsänger* who sang lines or stanzas which were then repeated by the group. The dancing was led by the *vortanzer* who, while the *vorsänger* sang, demonstrated a particular step which was then performed by all. At court performances it is probable that the minnesinger, the composer of the lyrics and the music, was both *vorsänger* and *vortanzer*, as well as his own accompanist. We do not know whether he was also the inventor of the dance movements, but, at any rate, it is clear that art and artists were less specialized in those days. The *reien* were summer dances which were performed in the open air, but there were other dances which were danced indoors. It is possible that some of these indoor and outdoor dances were similar to those still performed in various rural areas of Germany and Austria.

The favorite instruments for playing dance music, especially indoors, were the *fidel* and the *gîge*, which were also the most popular instruments for the accompaniment of the minnesong when there was no dancing. Both were stringed instruments, played with a bow and held against the shoulder, breast, or arm. Since they appear not to have been held by the chin in the modern manner, the performer was free to sing while playing them, though we do not know if the same player usually did both simultaneously. Other instruments included the lute, which came to Northern Europe during the Middle Ages from Moorish Spain, harps of various sizes, recorders, bells, triangles, and drums. Louder wind instruments – small horns, trumpets, shawms, chalumeaux, and bagpipes – were used for large festive occasions, ceremonials, and outdoor performances, though their use in connection with the minnesong must have been exceptional.

Whatever instruments were being used for a particular performance of minnesong, they were not specified in the manuscripts, and the parts they played were in various ways derived from the singer's part. They might double the voice part, improvise preludes and interludes in the song, or play varied versions of the melody simultaneously with the singer (heterophony), for although polyphony was common in other music of the same period, it is only at the very end of the minnesongs movement that there are any examples at all of polyphonic minnesong. Occasionally there are melismatic passages found in the manuscripts which may have been for the instruments to play, but generally, the performer was expected to devise his own part.

Almost all of the manuscripts which include music for the minnesong use staff notation, so that the pitch relationships are clearly indicated. The rhythm of the minnesong, is, however, not usually shown in the notation, though there are a very few late examples in which some rhythmic indications are present. The modern scholar is thus faced with the problem of determining what rhythmic solutions might have been used by the performers of minnesong. Most of the attempts to find a system for deducing the probable, or even possible, rhythm of minnesong have been based in some manner on the rhythm of the text. Unfortunately, however, when one examines the manuscripts of Spanish monophonic songs of the same period, one finds an astonishingly rich variety of rhythms, recorded in notation which does have exact rhythmic meaning. Since these rhythms are not at all dependent on the poetic meters, one may surmise that the noncommital notation of manuscripts elsewhere in Europe was actually interpreted by the singer in a manner which remains forever hidden from us and which cannot be reconstructed on the basis of the texts (Anglès, p. 48).

If, however, one does attempt to take the text as the basis for determining the musical rhythm, several solutions are possible. The accent of the text may be considered to produce a metrical pattern in the music in which the stressed and unstressed syllables are equal in length, but unequal in accent. On the other hand, if the stressed and unstressed parts of the foot are unequal in length, the stressed syllable becomes long and the poetic foot can conform to one of the rhythmic patterns of the rhythmic modes of the polyphonic music of the thirteenth century. A third possibility is that some form of free rhythm was used that could not be notated exactly (which would explain the use of such an inexact notation) and which could either change with each performer or be taught through oral tradition. This type of rhythm seems a particularly likely solution for songs in a florid style with many notes to each syllable: melismatic style (Anglès, p. 49).

It can be assumed that by far the greater part of the courtly songs which were composed during the period from the second half of the twelfth century to the middle of the fifteenth century have been lost. Many of them, no doubt, were never written down and existed only in an oral tradition; others, though recorded by the author, another performer, or a cleric, were subsequently lost; still others became so changed in the process of centuries of oral transmission that they are no longer recognizable as minnesongs. The greatest losses, unfortunately, occurred among the early songs, those which from the standpoint of both verse and music are the most interesting. In some cases songs have survived, but the names of their composers have not; in other instances the names of the composers are known to us, but all of their songs have been lost. Many minnesingers who had large repertoires are represented today by only one or two stanzas, and even some of the most famous, such as Heinrich von Morungen, have suffered severe losses. The loss of melodies has, of course, been far greater than that of lyrics, for while most of the minnesingers could record their verses, very few of them were able to write down their music. As a result, almost none of the twelfth century melodies has been preserved, and relatively few of those of the thirteenth century.

Of the lyrics and melodies which remain, many have suffered varying degrees of mutilation and distortion. In some of the extant manuscripts, words and even whole lines have been omitted, passages have been so distorted as to be incomprehensible, the musical notation has occasionally been changed, and sometimes stanzas have been added. In many cases songs which were composed by an unknown singer appear in the manuscripts under the name of a famous one. One of the most common causes for the corruption of the poetic text was the fact that the minnesong was recorded in a dialect that differed greatly from the one in which it was originally composed, so that what we now have is actually a translation and often not a very accurate one. The chief causes of corruption of the musical text were again that many tunes were preserved for a time only by oral transmission and that the nonmensural notation in which they were eventually recorded was inadequate. However, copyists' errors and deliberate changes in the texts also contributed. Nevertheless, in spite of losses, mutilations, and corruption, there are still several thousand minnesong texts extant in a good state of preservation. They represent the work of some 150 composers. Although the loss of melodies was even more severe, there are still approximately 450 minnesong tunes extant, enough to present a fairly adequate picture of the music of the minnesingers. Even the surviving musical texts, however, give little indication of the improvised ornamentation which the singers used to embellish and vary their performances, and which may be the source of some of the variant versions in the surviving melodies. Unfortunately, very few of the minnesongs exist in variant versions of the melodies, so the comparison which is so fruitful in the study of many Romance tunes is not possible with the minnesongs.

It is difficult to generalize about the life or position of a minnesinger, for this designation is applied to all who composed and sang songs dealing with courtly love, *minne*. It may also include those who used the form and language of the minnesong to treat subjects other than *minne*. The minnesingers came from many classes of society. Among them were an emperor, the Hohenstaufen Heinrich VI, and eight other ruling princes, the last of whom was Wizlaw. There were some dozen counts and about sixty nobles of the *Ministerial* class, commonly known as knights. From the middle of the thirteenth century on, the ranks of the minnesingers were swelled by about thirty middle-class singers and several clerics. The largest and most representative group was that of the minor nobility, but even within this group there were great variations with regard to wealth and position. Friedrich von Hausen was wealthy and a prominent man of his day; Walther von der Vogelweide was a penniless wanderer who was dependent on his songs for his livelihood. As the minnesong developed and then declined, the general trend with regard to rank and importance of its singers was steadily downward. The first generation of minnesingers all belonged to the propertied nobility; the chief representatives of the second generation were impecunious nobility who had become professional entertainers; commoners appeared in the third generation, and their numbers gradually increased until at its end the minnesong was completely taken over by middle-class artisans, the meistersingers.

The minnesong had its beginning in the compositions of Austrian noblemen who began to write about the middle of the twelfth century. From the South it spread to the Rhineland area and then to Middle Germany. North Germany, because of its political, economic and linguistic isolation, contributed little to the minnesong; indeed, Wizlaw is its only important minnesinger.

Most of the minnesingers of all ranks and stations traveled widely. Wars, crusades, politics, family affairs, tournaments, and festivals took the princes and wealthy nobility on many journeys; necessity and wanderlust drove the penniless from court to court. Thus the minnesongs and the reputations of their singers were spread throughout the German-speaking lands. The chief centers of the minnesongs were those courts where there was a great deal of social life and entertainment. Particularly renowned in this respect were those of the Swabian Hohenstaufens, the dukes of Babenberg in Vienna, Margrave Dietrich of Meissen, and, most famous and boisterous of all, that of Count Hermann of Thuringia. At these courts and others gathered for the first time in German history a rather large, aristocratic leisure class which required a considerable amount of entertaining. There were hunts, tournaments, dances, evenings devoted to singing, and whole weeks taken up with the narration of one or another of the courtly epics of the day.

On a minnesong evening a group of knights and ladies would amuse themselves by performing their own compositions or listening to those of a professional composer and singer. The singer would sometimes accompany himself with a stringed instrument, and sometimes be accompanied by one or more instrumentalists. The performer was an actor and mimic as well as a singer and his song was delivered with gestures, sighs, winks, dramatic facial expressions, and pauses and hesitations, all of which affected both verse and music. The fact that the minnesong was above all a performance, which the composer-singer may have varied from time to time and which subsequent performers may have altered frequently before either words or music were recorded, sometimes makes it impossible to ascertain definitely the intent of the composer. It may be that some of the songs which appear to be filled with pain and sorrow were sung with a knowing smile or in a comically exaggerated manner, so that what seems to be tragic is actually comic. It is at least certain that there was a considerable amount of intentional and witty ambiguity and playing with words in the minnesong, almost from its beginning.

Wizlaw was one of the last significant composers of minnesongs and, although isolated from what had been the chief centers of compositon, was apparently quite familiar with the tradition as a whole as well as with many individual works of his predecessors. And, even though he wrote many years after the classical period of the minnesong, his works do not differ essentially in mood, expression, content, and form from those which had been written a century earlier. His songs are, of course, colored by his individual personality, but are in most respects representative of the general minnesong tradition.

CHAPTER THREE

THE *SPRÜCHE*

With regard to content and expression Wizlaw's *Sprüche* are quite traditional. His subject matter is that most characteristic of *Spruch* verse in general: religious teaching, moral advice, parable, legend, riddle, and eulogy. Several of the themes are taken from the Bible and most of the stanzas contain some biblical or religious reference. If there is anything atypical in the poems, it is a trace of the light-hearted optimism and humor which is so characteristic of his minnesongs. The *Sprüche* are, however, inferior to the minnesongs; indeed one critic, O. Knoop, referred to them as schoolboy exercises. But this judgment is too harsh, for they are certainly superior to most of the *Spruch* verse which has been preserved. It is true that they show little originality of expression and contain metrical imperfections, not all of which can be blamed on the carelessness of the scribe. On the other hand, Wizlaw demonstrates in these songs for the most part an ability to use a complicated metrical and rhyme pattern in a smooth and facile manner. If they were indeed schoolboy exercises, the schoolboy was one who showed great promise.

The *Sprüche* of Wizlaw appear in five different *Töne*, that is, in five different stanzaic patterns and melodies, assuming that one *Spruch* of disputed authorship is by him. This *Spruch* is incomplete and is the only one using its specific *Ton*. The first nine *Sprüche* which are definitely by Wizlaw have the same *Ton*, *Spruch* X and *Spruch* XI are in another *Ton*, and the last two have each its own *Ton*. The disputed *Spruch* contains only the two *Stollen*, rhyming *a b c d* : *a b c d* and two lines of the *Abgesang*. It has dimeter, tetrameter, and hexameter lines. Since this *Spruch* has only recently been attributed to Wizlaw, it will not be counted in the enumeration of the *Sprüche* so that the traditional designations of *Sprüche* and *Spruch*-melodies may be preserved.

The poetic form of the first *Ton* which is definitely by Wizlaw is moderately complex. It has an *Aufgesang* of two *Stollen*, each consisting of a couplet and a third line which rhymes with the third line of the other *Stollen* as well as the last line of the *Abgesang*. The *Abgesang* has a similar form. It has a couplet and a third line which rhymes with its counterpart above, and a final group of three lines which repeat the form of the *Stollen*. The *Spruch*, therefore, consists of five groups of three lines each, the first, second and fifth of which are alike in metrical form and have the same melody. The third and fourth groups have the same rhyme pattern as the others, but the lines are shorter. The melody for these two groups is through-composed and is not the same as that of the *Stollen*.

The second *Ton*, that in which *Spruch* X and *Spruch* XI are composed, employs essentially the same pattern as the first *Ton*, even though line lengths and rhyme scheme are different. Of particular interest is the fact that the fifth section of the *Spruch* has neither the same rhyme scheme nor the same line lengths as the two *Stollen*, and yet it has the same melody as they do. The melody fits because there is the same total number of accented syllables in the fifth section as in each of the first two sections. It is a rather rare case in which there is a repeat of the musical *Stollen* without a faithful repetition of the poetic *Stollen*.

The poetic form of the third *Ton*, that in which *Spruch* XII is composed, is identical with that of the first *Ton*, except for line lengths. Musically it is even more symmetrical than is the first *Ton*, in that the third and fourth sections of the stanza are not through-composed, but repeat the same melody, which, however, differs from that of the other three sections.

The verse structure of the fourth *Ton* is much simpler and is quite unlike the other three. It consists of an *Aufgesang* and an *Abgesang*, but the latter is not divisible into sections and does not end in a repeat of the *Stollen*. The stanza, therefore, consists of three, rather than of five parts.

Not only the scholar who criticized them, but other scholars, including Ettmüller and Pyl, have suggested that the *Sprüche* were composed when Wizlaw was quite young, perhaps while he was still a pupil of Der Ungelarde. The repetition of ideas and expressions, the irregularities in meter, the borrowings from other singers, and the use of rather hackneyed and trite themes all seem to point to the work of a young and inexperienced poet. They might also indicate the influence of a pedantic, bourgeois schoolmaster.

It is rather disappointing that Wizlaw, unlike many of the composers of *Sprüche* reveals little of himself or of his personal experiences in these verses. The *Spruch* of uncertain authorship is a hymn of praise to God and expresses the complete dependence of man upon divinity. Its theme is the most common in the didactic verse of the period. *Spruch* I, however, which discusses the general deterioration of the culture (a favorite topic of *Spruch* poets from Walther von der Vogelweide on), may refer to a contemporary event that affected Wizlaw directly. The comments about the relations between fathers and sons could have been inspired by the troubles in the country of Werle, in which Wizlaw's father became so unfortunately involved. The disorders began with a feud between Heinrich I, the ruler, and his two sons. When the father died (1291) during the hostilities, his sons were driven out of their land by their cousins and fled to Rügen, where they received protection and aid from Wizlaw's father. This *Spruch* differs from the others which were sung to the same melody in two respects: the repeated *Stollen* at the end employs feminine, rather than masculine rhyme, and the last line lacks one metrical foot.

Spruch II deals with the Virgin Mary and the incarnation of Christ, a subject treated by many of the *Spruch* poets. An interesting medieval literary conceit is contained in the salutation of the angel Gabriel when he addresses the Virgin with 'Ave, blessed Mary!' The angel designates her as the reversed or transformed Eva (English Eve), for, as death and sin came into the world by the act of Eva, so life and salvation are brought to us through Ave, or Mary. Other singers, including Wizlaw's friend Frauenlob, employed the Latin salutation in a similar way, and Wizlaw's listeners would have recognized immediately his play on words.

The parables of Jesus served as an important source for the didactic verse of the minnesingers. However, the story of the man who built his house upon the sand, which introduces *Spruch* III, was apparently not used by any other minnesinger, although it does appear frequently in other medieval literature. The song is a good example of the symmetry of thought which is basic to all works of the courtly poets. In general, the content of the first *Stollen* parallels or contrasts with the content of the second *Stollen*, and together they present the situation. The *Abgesang* offers a resolution of that situation. In the first *Stollen* of this *Spruch* the singer tells of how he built a house on the sand, but there was no firm support and the house falls. In the second *Stollen* the house is resting in a filthy pool when God comes and raises it up with his hand. Thus, the thoughtless builder, the sand, the lack of support, and the falling of the first *Stollen* are contrasted in turn with omniscient God, the filthy pool, God's hand, and the raising up of the second *Stollen*. The *Abgesang* resolves the contrast with a hymn of praise to Almighty God.

The source of *Spruch* IV is the story which Livy tells in Book VII, Chapter 6, of his history of Rome. According to Livy a volcano opened up in the city and Marcus Curtius sprang into it to appease the wrath of the gods and save the city. Wizlaw, however, has him wait for a year before sacrificing himself, during which time the grateful Romans gave him everything he wished, including beautiful women. The passage in the Latin version, 'donaque ac fruges super eum a multitudine uirorum ac mulierum congestas,' may have given Wizlaw a hint for his account. In any case, it is characteristic of Wizlaw's affirmation of the sensual joys of life, as well as his sense of humor, that he should allow his hero to be abundantly rewarded beforehand for his heroism. Although, according to Knoop, this is the only appearance of Marcus Curtius in extant medieval literature, it is quite possible that Wizlaw's immediate source was not Livy, but rather some medieval intermediary whose work has since vanished.

Spruch V is a riddle in verse and the listeners were supposed to guess the answer after the singer had finished. Such rhymed riddles were doubtless prevalent in German folk literature long before it began to be recorded, and the minnesingers, for all of their sophistication, frequently used popular material for their songs. Several solutions have been suggested for this riddle, the most plausible of which (Pyl, p. 47) turns upon the ambiguity of the Low German word *blod*, which can mean either 'blood,' 'blossom,' or 'foolish.' *Blod* with the meaning 'blood' carries with it the connotations of passion (hot-blooded), bravery (red-blooded), nobility (blue-blooded), as well as generosity (warm-blooded or warm-hearted). The object of the riddle has all of these characteristics and is, in addition, smaller than a pea (a blossom) and gives advice though it is stupid (foolish). If the answer is *blod*, then the riddle itself must have been restricted to the Low German area, for no similar ambiguity existed in Middle High German.

Spruch VI is a prayer and resembles in content, language and form several Protestant hymns of the sixteenth century. This resemblance is not necessarily mere coincidence, for just as many of the lovesongs of the minnesingers doubtless reappeared in a simplified form as folksongs, it is likewise probable that some of their *Sprüche* were subsequently adapted to congregational hymns, particularly during the Reformation. Indeed, it would not be surprising if some of our modern hymnals should contain works by one or another medieval minnesinger. One such instance may be Luther's chorale *Aus tiefer Not*, which in its Lutheran form dates from 1524. The tune bears a striking resemblance to a metrical setting of the 130th Psalm in a meistersinger manuscript (Tübingen, Universitätsbibliothek, Depot der ehem. Preuss. Staatsbibliothek, Ms. germ 25, f. 12) where it is attributed to Konrad von Würzburg, an early thirteenth century minnesinger.

Daniel's account of the dream of Nebuchadnezzar provides the subject matter for *Spruch* VII. This story was quite popular among medieval writers and was treated by several minnesingers prior to Wizlaw. The version of a certain Meister Kelin deviates greatly from the Biblical account. He tells that the king in his dream saw three worlds, one of gold, another of silver, a third of iron, and then adds that his own age is that of copper. Der Marner, a highly educated singer-priest, tells the story very nearly as Daniel does, but goes on to interpret it according to his own time: the present is the iron age, he says, and the clay feet are the ruling princes. The middle-class singer, Rumsland, gives the most detailed explication of the dream. After having told the story according to Daniel, he goes on to say that the golden head is Christianity; for through baptism man is cleansed and is as pure as gold. If, however, he is separated from God, he is gradually degraded, resembling first silver, then brass, then iron, and finally receives feet of clay. At last he is crushed by a stone which rolls from the nearby mountain. The stone is Jesus and the mountain from which it comes is Mary. The first stanza of Wizlaw's *Spruch* is so like that of Rumsland, whose song appears in the same manuscript as the songs of Wizlaw, that one can assume that the latter used it as a model. Wizlaw's second stanza, however, is more like Der Marner's, in that he generalizes about the gradual decline of the world. This is the only one of Wizlaw's *Sprüche* which has two stanzas. The dream and the interpretation together were apparently too much to be treated within the limits of this *Ton*, and a longer stanza would have necessitated the composition of a new melody.

In *Spruch* VIII Wizlaw attacks the passive attitude that accepts whatever comes with the excuse that all is predestined. The similarity of his song to one by Reinmar von Zweter (ca. 1200 - ca. 1260) is close enough in form as well as content for one to be sure that Wizlaw was familiar with the work of the older singer. In his song, *Beschaffen und ez muoste sein* (von der Hagen, II, 188), Reinmar, too, warns against a blind belief in fate and against attempts to blame fate for one's own shortcomings and failures. The rather sharp tone which Wizlaw employs here is more characteristic of Reinmar's uncompromising morality than of his own geniality.

Spruch IX is a eulogy of a knight of Holstein, the identity of whom has not been definitely established. Some of the scholars who have treated Wizlaw believed that the question of identity is answered in the song itself. A literal translation of the fourth line of the Jena Manuscript version would be 'him I have named to you,' and this has led scholars to seek this name in the first three lines. The word 'noble' in the second line appears in the original text as *eren rich*, which is close enough to the name Erich for some to accuse Wizlaw of a pun and declare the hero of the verses to be an Erich of Holstein. Unfortunately for this theory, however, the records of Holstein, which are quite complete for the period in question, tell of no Erich among its nobility. Another solution to the problem has been to assume that the scribe made an error in line three and wrote *wert* (worthy) instead of *Gerd*, a short form of Gerhard. Considering the carelessness of the scribe, such an assumption has some merit, especially since there was a well-known and colorful Gerhard of Holstein whom Wizlaw doubtless knew. However, this Gerhard was some twenty-seven years younger than Wizlaw and the latter would have been about fifty at the time of the composition of the song, if Gerhard was actually its subject. And the texts of the *Sprüche* strongly indicate that they were composed by a young man. A second reason for rejecting this theory is that Wizlaw's songs were still being sung when the Jena Manuscript was written and the fame of Gerhard was still wide-spread. To assume that the scribe could have recorded the song under these conditions and left out the name of its hero is a little far-fetched. Finally, it makes little sense for Wizlaw to name his hero in one line and then, in the following line, tell us that he has named him. If we assume such a scribal error in line three, then line four is quite superfluous.

Two other explanations of Wizlaw's comment in line four, which have been completely overlooked, are more plausible than either of those mentioned. One is that Wizlaw may have sung of the knight of Holstein in a previous *Spruch* which has been lost. The other is that the piece was composed and sung by Wizlaw on the occasion of a visit of this knight. If the knight was present at the performance and had been previously introduced to the other guests by his host, there would have been little need to give his name in the song. After all, Wizlaw, like the other minnesingers, composed and sang for his immediate audience, not for posterity.

In *Spruch* X, a didactic song which compares the good and honorable man with the wicked wretch, the influence of Reinmar von Zweter is once more apparent. The latter's *Sage, ungelopter richer man* (von der Hagen, II, 188) has the same theme, and the correspondence of several phrases is sufficiently close that one may be sure that Wizlaw knew Reinmar's song. It is even possible that it was a part of Wizlaw's performance repertoire. At the same time it must be said that the general content of both songs is to be found in the *Sprüche* of several other composers, including in particular one by Friedrich von Sonnenburg (von der Hagen, III, 70).

Spruch XI expresses the repentance of the singer for his errors and weakness and calls upon God to strengthen him. However, it should not be assumed that this was a purely personal confession, for just as the minnesinger through his compositions and performances supplied a need on the part of his audience for romance, sorrow, and suffering, so did he also vicariously repent for them. The repentance song, the Latin *canticum poenitentiam testans*, was a popular type of song in the Middle Ages, to which most of the better-known minnesingers contributed. It does not differ greatly from our modern hymn; however, whereas we confine our hymn singing to church services, the medieval audiences welcomed such compositions in secular performances. The favorite occasion for the singing of repentence songs was Easter and, considering Wizlaw's reference to 'this most holy day,' we can assume that the first performance of this work was at a secular celebration of Easter.

In *Spruch* XII Wizlaw calls down the wrath of the Lord on the most frequently condemned villain of medieval song, the malicious gossip. In the love songs of the minnesingers it is he who presents the greatest threat to the happiness of the knight and lady and it is principally because of him that their meetings must be secret. In the *Sprüche* it is the malicious gossip who attacks the knight where he is most sensitive in that he attempts to deprive the latter of merited fame and honor. Wizlaw prays that the scoundrel may receive the ultimate penalty, the scorn of men and the ridicule of women.

The last of Wizlaw's *Sprüche*, *Spruch* XIII, though not at all original in content, is decidedly the best, and is the only one of the *Sprüche* to rank poetically with his minnesongs. In the singer's brief advice to the youth there is a simplicity of language and a sincerity of expression of moral and religious truths which transcends the trite didacticism of the theme. Although many of the minnesingers have given advice to the younger generation, few, if any, have done it so well.

CHAPTER FOUR

THE MINNESONGS

The minnesong tradition in which Wizlaw composed was very restrictive with regard to content, attitude, and expression and, in spite of the emphasis on originality of form, custom demanded that even here the poet should confine himself to certain general structural patterns. Nevertheless Wizlaw's songs are not mere stereotypes. Lurking behind all the accumulated traditions in his works is a lively personality which gives them a character of their own. They are distinguished by light-hearted humor and by a joyful affirmation of sensual pleasure. They reflect an active enjoyment of color: green fields and forests, bright flowers, gay clothing, and red cheeks and lips; of sound: the music of birds and strings; of smell: the scent of flowers from the body of his loved one; of movement: dancing and jousting; and of taste: wine, mead, and well-fattened swine. To be sure, the traditional aspects of *minne* are mentioned – constancy, longing, and sorrow – but in general Wizlaw was no languishing lover who devoted his life to the service of a haughty and unresponsive lady. He was essentially a pagan Epicurean upon whom the heritage of four generations of Christian asceticism still rested lightly.

Some scholars have explained that which is most distinctive of Wizlaw, what Nietzsche called the Dionysian element, on a historical basis, by pointing to the decline and corruption of chivalric ideals since the early thirteenth century. However, such an explanation ignores the fact that many individual songs of the twelfth and early thirteenth century reveal a spirit quite similar to that which is characteristic of Wizlaw. Wizlaw was as saturated with the ideals of chivalry as any of the earlier singers, but, as a ruling prince and very eligible bachelor during his productive years, he would not be as likely to sing of hopeless love as would a penniless wanderer. And, even in his later life when his principality was practically bankrupt, he was always able to afford most of the luxuries that his sensual nature enjoyed. The distinctive character of Wizlaw's verse must be explained by his personality and his station in life, not by his times. Though a belated minnesinger, he was not a decadent one.

It is quite in keeping with Wizlaw's light-hearted spirit that he should have composed primarily dance songs with nature introductions. The nature introduction appears in the earliest minnesongs and, although it has antecedents in medieval Latin verse, doubtless originated with the songs sung at pagan spring festivals. Most of the nature introductions which appear in minnesongs describe the joys and beauty of spring; however, some also portray summer, fall, and winter scenes. The popularity of the nature introduction declined during the latter part of the twelfth century, but was revived during the thirteenth century by Neidhart von Reuenthal, Gottfried von Neifen, Burkhart von Hohenfels, and Ulrich von Winterstetten. From this time on it remained an important element in the minnesong tradition. However, none of the more prominent minnesingers, with the exception of Neidhart, is as closely identified with the nature introduction as is Wizlaw. Indeed, the nature introduction plays a more prominent role in Wizlaw's songs than in those of any other minnesinger, taking up about half of the song. The content of Wizlaw's dance songs is arranged in general as follows: the first stanza tells of the loveliness of spring, the second stanza compares (either directly or by implication) this beauty with that of women, the third and last stanza sings of the relation between a particular woman and the poet. In the works of most minnesingers this stanza would pour forth the laments of a lover whose lady does not reward loyalty or return his affection. However, Wizlaw seems to have been more fortunate than most. Within this set pattern Wizlaw depends upon uniqueness of *Ton*, variety of expression, and originality of similes and metaphors to give distinction to each individual song.

The dance songs with nature introductions describing spring and summer were traditionally sung as accompaniment to *reien*, the lively group dances which were performed in the open air. We should imagine Wizlaw's spring songs as having been sung in the enclosed courtyard of one or another of his castles while his guests, attired in the colorful costumes which he describes in one of his songs, leaped merrily about at the direction of the dancing master. Since he doubtless employed a number of court musicians, the songs could have been accompanied by instrumentalists.

Although there is something unique in Wizlaw's songs, there is a great deal more that is traditional. In his nature introductions he nowhere mentions the landscape he knew: the sea, the chalk cliffs of the island of Rügen, the salt marshes of the coastland. He describes the same stereotyped nature about which courtly poets had sung for over a century. The lady, too, is not an individual, but is the same indistinct personality with the same virtues and physical attractions whom hundreds of other minnesingers had loved. There is the traditional personification of Sir May, Sir Winter and Lady Love, and (occasionally) the traditional love-lorn knight who voices his age-old lament. This lack of individualized characterization does not represent a weakness in Wizlaw any more than it does in other minnesingers. It is actually a positive factor in a stylized, symbolic art which stressed form and symmetry, rather than individuality. What distinguished the greater minnesingers was not that they freed themselves of the restrictions of the minnesong conventions, but that they created verse which was pleasing and in its own way unique while remaining within the strict limits of the genre.

One of the most distinctive characteristics of a minnesong is the relationship it reveals between the performer and his audience. This relationship varies from the situation in which the song takes no cognizance of an audience to one in which the performer frequently and familiarly addresses his audience, refers to himself as a performer, and even discusses with the audience the performance itself. Some of Wizlaw's songs indicate a frank awareness that he is not singing directly of an experience, but is singing a *song* about an experience, that is, that he is consciously entertaining. He addresses his audience, speaks of himself as a performer, and discusses the song as a performance. However, he does not approach buffoonery as do some of the minnesingers. There is always a certain reserve in his relationship to his listeners and they would have been constantly aware that the singer was not a jester of the court, but its master. Some of the Romantic critics of the nineteenth century have speculated as to the identity of the lady of whom Wizlaw sings. One mentions his first wife, Margarete, another suggests that he was in love with a commoner and that this relationship explains his late marriage and his apparent reluctance to marry at all. However, it is not at all necessary for us to assume the appearance of any real woman in the songs; like his modern counterpart, Wizlaw composed not for an individual, but for a public.

Structurally, Wizlaw's minnesongs are composed of an *Aufgesang* and an *Abgesang* which sometimes ended with a repeat of the *Stollen* melody. In most instances there are three stanzas. Since minnesongs, except those of the earliest period, traditionally have three or more stanzas, one may assume in the case of three of Wizlaw's four shorter songs that stanzas have been lost.

The single one-stanza minnesong that is probably complete is the one which appears first in the manuscript. It is a simple and sincere declaration of love which produces such an impression of unity and completeness that one cannot imagine what the poet would have left to say in other stanzas. He addresses the lady directly, there is no hint of a performance or an audience, and one feels that, if any of Wizlaw's songs were intended for a particular person, it would be this one. It is perhaps significant that Wizlaw uses the word 'faithfulness' here and in no other song. In the original it is the best of his compositions and one of the best in the entire minnesong repertoire. In the passage where Wizlaw invokes the protection of God for his loved-one there is an echo of a song by his contemporary and neighbor, Otto IV, Margrave of Brandenburg (Kraus, I, 317), but it is not strong enough to indicate a literary influence.

The minnesong which appears next in the manuscript is the most controversial of Wizlaw's songs. In a single stanza the singer tells of having heard a beautiful melody by Der Ungelarde, bewails his own inadequacy as a poet, and discusses the difficulty of composition. The controversy centers about the question as to whether the work is really a love song. One scholar in particular, von der Hagen, maintains that it is not, and suggests that the song is either merely the lament of the poet that he cannot compose a good poem to the melody which he has heard, or that the song itself is a beginner's attempt to compose lyrics in a very difficult *Ton* which he has borrowed from Der Ungelarde but cannot handle very well. According to the latter interpretation the melody of the song is not by Wizlaw at all, but by Der Ungelarde. It seems more probable, however, that the melody is by Wizlaw, that the song is a love song, and that its meaning is as follows. The poet has heard the song of Der Ungelarde, but at first cannot do as well himself because he has never suffered the pangs of love. Later he learns to know love's pain and with it discovers the secret of composing love songs. He praises Der Ungelarde, for he now realizes what suffering the latter must have endured in order to be able to compose such a beautiful song. One should assume that the one extant stanza is only an introduction to the story of the singer's unhappy love affair which was related in two subsequent stanzas that have been lost. This song is the only link between Wizlaw and the Magister Ungelarde of Stralsund. The latter has also been mentioned by the Nürnberg barber and meistersinger Hans Folz (ca. 1433-1513), and five stanzas in the *Kolmar Liederhandschrift*, a collection of meistersongs, have been erroneously ascribed to him by the meistersingers.

Minnesong III is a traditional lover's plaint which tells of the joys and sorrows of love, describes the wondrous beauty and charm of the lady, and relates how Cupid's arrow has struck him, kindled fires within him, and deprived him of his reason. There is a possible ambiguity in this song too. The first line speaks of a lamenting song, but it is not entirely clear as to whether the poet means the song which follows or one which has been previously sung, perhaps that discussed above. The musicologist Gennrich apparently believes that the reference is to the melody of Der Ungelarde, for he attempts to prove by analysis of the music that Minnesong III is a contrafact, that is, a poem composed to a borrowed tune. However, his evidence seems insufficient. At any rate, it is probable that the lamenting song is the one which Wizlaw is singing at the time. Wizlaw's familiarity with minnesong literature is indicated by the fact that the first line of his second stanza coincides almost exactly with the beginning of a song which has been erroneously ascribed to King Wenzel I of Bohemia (1205-1253), a patron of minnesingers (Kraus, I, 584). It should be noted in Minnesong III that the author employs his most distinctive device, the linking of the two *Stollen* and the *Abgesang* by means of a final rhyme.

In Minnesong IV Wizlaw gives an example of the dawn song. In its earliest form this type of minnesong consisted of a dialogue between a knight and a lady who must part at break of day after a night of love. Before the end of the twelfth century, however, a third figure was added, that of the watchman, a friend of the lovers, who wakes them on his morning round. He thus helps to thwart the lady's guardians who, although they never appear openly, always lurk ominously in the background. The birds who sing at dawn make up another traditional element of the dawn song, one that is important musically because some of the later composers, including Wizlaw, incorporate their notes into the melody. The first four lines of the first stanza of this song are missing in the manuscript, but since the dawn song had become highly standardized by Wizlaw's time, it is not at all difficult to reconstruct approximately the poetic text. Unfortunately, there is no way to reconstruct the music which is missing.

The most remarkable characteristic of the minnesingers as artists was their strong feeling for form and symmetry: in music, in metrics, and in content. Metrically the symmetry of Minnesong V is based on the number three. Each of the three stanzas consists of three *Stollen*, the third line of which (the linking line) contains three feet. In order to give more weight to the *Abgesang*, the part in which a situation is resolved, the third *Stollen* of the stanza is preceded by a single line, which also has three feet. The song, a lover's plaint, also shows symmetry in its use of point of view, which once more is based on the number three. In the first stanza the knight speaks of himself in the first person and of the lady in the third person. In the second stanza he addresses the lady in the second person and refers to himself in the third person. In the final stanza he uses the first person for himself and the second person for the lady, thus giving it a more dynamic quality than the preceding stanzas. Other examples of symmetry are also apparent in the song.

The rest of Wizlaw's songs are songs of the seasons, dance tunes with nature introductions. Songs VI, VII, IX, X, and XI are May songs, VIII and XII are winter songs, and XIII is a fall or harvest song. Although these are all love songs, in only VII and XI is there more than a mere hint of a lover's lament, and even in these two the lover's situation is by no means hopeless.

Minnesong VI describes a village green in May, bright with the colors of leaves, flowers, birds, and the gay spring costumes, decked with garlands of flowers, of those who have gathered there for a dance. The cheeks of the ladies are like rubies on the snow and the whole colorful scene reminds the singer of a magnificent tapestry. It is no wonder that he thinks of his lady and the delights of her love. Technically the work is quite interesting. The stanzas have a *Stollen* rhyme of *a a a b* and an *Abgesang* rhyme of *d d e e e*, thus the rhyme of the *Abgesang*, with the addition of a line, is just the reverse of that of the *Stollen*.

In the following minnesong Wizlaw paints a similar, and even gayer scene of happy dancing on the common, and names himself as the singer. The fact that he calls himself 'Wizlaw, the Younger,' indicates that the song was composed before the death of his father. The stanzas have a complicated structure, with dimeter, trimeter, tetrameter, and pentameter lines, and an intricate rhyme pattern. The *Stollen* rhyme is *a a a a b* and that part of the *Abgesang* which precedes the repeated Stollen rhymes *d e d f f*, with the *e*-line rhyming with the last line of the repeated *Stollen*, eight lines later. The modern listener would probably miss this delayed rhyme entirely, but the ear of the medieval audience was more retentive. In one minnesong, not by Wizlaw, every eleventh line rhymes.

In several respects Minnesong VIII is rather unique among

the winter songs of the minnesingers. Those composed by the penniless wandering minstrels are often quite gloomy and reflect their own sufferings from the harsh elements. But Wizlaw, although he voices the traditional complaint about the cold, is chiefly distressed because in winter the women conceal their pretty dresses with heavy, drab coats. For the most part he is well satisfied with winter, for he finds the long nights of love to be a more than adequate compensation for the loss of the delights of summer. These joys of consummated love are a rather unusual subject for a minnesong and ordinarily appear only in songs about knights and peasant girls. The object of Wizlaw's affection, however, is a lady. Metrically the song is distinguished for its very effective use of monometer lines and its ingenious linking of stanzas by the rhyming of the last word of one stanza with the first word of the following one.

In Minnesong IX Wizlaw once more sings of the joys rather than of the sorrows of love, and does so with exuberance and baroque extravagance. He employs his most highly involved *Ton*, one which is unsurpassed in complexity, even in a period when poets especially prided themselves on metrical virtuosity. Most of the lines are tetrameter, with one dimeter and one hexameter line per stanza. Those beginning with an unaccented syllable end with a masculine rhyme, while those beginning with an accented syllable end with a feminine rhyme, thus producing dactyls at regular intervals in a basically iambic rhythm. However, it is in his rhyme scheme that Wizlaw shows particular ingenuity. By using dashes to indicate the position of unrhymed feet, the rhyme scheme may be reproduced as follows:

Stollen   – – – a
                  – – – a
                  a – – b

```
Stollen      - - - c
             - - - c
             c - - b
Abgesang     d d d - - e
             e e
             - - - - - f
             - f.
```

From the standpoint of poetry alone one might well object that such metrical virtuosity must seem pretentious and detract from the effectiveness of the work. However, it must be remembered that a minnesong is sung and, since it is communicated through a double medium, it cannot be compared to a non-composed poem any more than an opera libretto should be compared to a drama. Libretti need to be exaggerated in order to stand out from the music, and the virtuosity of a minnesong often gave the performer excellent opportunities for effective and varied expression. The mention of hills in the nature introduction of Minnesong IX suggests that it may have been composed on the island of Rügen. The mainland area of Wizlaw's principality consisted of a lowland plain.

The two May songs X and XI are chiefly distinctive for their bold reference to the goal of the singer's frankly sexual desires, a goal which traditionally is carefully veiled with polite, but suggestive ambiguities. In the latter song there is even the most unconventional threat that the singer may resort, if necessary, to sovereign prerogatives. The best element of Minnesong X is the simple and appealing portrayal of the lady's feeling of pride in knowing that she is beautiful in her fine clothes and that everyone is admiring her. Of particular interest in Minnesong XI are the brief description of a tournament and the subsequent festivities and the clever, if slightly naughty, play on the word 'jousting.' With regard to form Minnesong X is unusual in its regularity. Thematically as well as structurally the *Abgesang* resembles the *Aufgesang*, thus giving the impression of a stanza made up solely of four *Stollen*.

The second of Wizlaw's two winter songs, Minnesong XII, consists of only two stanzas, but it is obvious that one stanza, the last one, has been lost. The song is relatively simple in both form and language. The singer regrets the loss of summer's leaves and flowers, but feels fully compensated for them by the roses on the cheeks and lips of his lady and the fragrance of blossoms and summer breezes which comes from her. The trochaic meter, with occasional dactyls, produces a somewhat staccato rhythm and one can imagine that the steps which were danced to it were livelier than those of most indoor dances.

The tone of Wizlaw's only fall song, Minnesong XIII, is quite different from the rest. The single extant stanza, which is not quite complete, describes in a realistic, unadorned manner the simple joys of harvest time: the beer and wine, the fat geese and pigs, the cackling of chickens and the fishing in the brooks. Although one can assume that the missing stanzas introduced a love element, there is little here of the sophisticated expression of the conventional minnesong. There are two explanations for the distinctive tone of the song. One deals with the nature of the harvest festival itself. Although its origins are as remote in the Germanic past as those of the spring festival, it was never fully adopted and refined by courtly society and was treated only rarely by courtly singers until the latter part of the fourteenth century when the Monk of Salzburg began to compose. The harvest song, therefore, remained to some extent a forthright peasant song, even in the hands of a sophisticated composer. The tone of the song can also be explained on the basis of literary influence, for Wizlaw obviously drew from a well-known drinking song, *Sit si mir niht lonen wil*, of the Swiss singer, Steinmar von Klingenau (ca. 1230 – ca. 1290). Steinmar's song has a rough and earthy flavor which could have been transmitted in part to Wizlaw's verses. The extant stanza lacks either 1½ or 2½ lines, depending upon whether one judges by the poetic or the musical structure. If one uses the latter criterion, the missing part of the melody can be reconstructed.

Thirteen minnesongs are not many with which to establish a reputation as a poet and composer, but the quality of Wizlaw's compositions is consistently high. And, although they treat traditional themes and situations, Wizlaw's lighthearted nature, strong sensuousness, and unexcelled ability to compose smoothly in a highly complex metrical and rhyme structure give them a distinctive character. His minnesongs do not rank with the best of Walther von der Vogelweide, Heinrich von Morungen or Neidhart von Reuenthal, but are nevertheless far superior to those of the majority of the minnesingers. They can be read and heard with pleasure even in this modern age which has such different standards for excellence in song. Actually, although as a poet Wizlaw is almost unknown even to those who are interested in the minnesong, as a composer he is by no means forgotten and his songs appear in a number of nineteenth and twentieth century anthologies of early German music.

CHAPTER FIVE

THE MELODIES

Wizlaw's melodies exhibit a variety of styles, ranging from the austere repetition of simple, short melodic formulas, as in Minnesong VII, to the melismatic text-painting of Minnesong IV, a dawn song with singing birds. Some of the songs have vigorous, jaunty, folk-like melodies (Minnesong V); others display a wealth of melodic ornamentation which suggests a freer, more sophisticated style of performance. The embellished style finds its most complex expression, surprisingly enough, not in the minnesongs, but in the *Sprüche*, particularly *Spruch* XIII.

Since a variety of styles is found in the melodies, a method of transcription of the rhythm which is satisfactory for one style seems forced in others. Higini Anglès has shown that in the medieval songs which use mensural notation a consistent system of rhythmic notation is found most commonly in songs which have a syllabic style (Anglès, p. 45). Melismatic songs appear to have been performed in a manner which could not be represented accurately in the notation. On the basis of such evidence as is available it seems that the minnesingers used a variety of rhythmic renderings of different styles of songs; therefore, different types of rhythmic transcription appropriate to the variety in the styles of Wizlaw's songs have been used in this work. The songs which have a regular syllabic style (*Spruch* XII and all of the minnesongs except II and IV) have been transcribed in exact rhythms. These songs could all be sung in duple meter for a smooth, flowing manner of performance. A transcription in the first rhythmic mode ($\frac{3}{4}$ ♩ ♩) could be used for all of the same songs, producing a more strongly marked rhythm. In the songs in which several neumes fall on unaccented syllables, with single notes falling mainly on accented syllables, the second rhythmic mode ($\frac{3}{4}$ ♩ ♫) can be used in the transcription, though as in Minnesong V, the possibility of using the third

CHART I

The Equivalents In Modern Notation Of The Rhythmic Modes

Mode I $\frac{3}{4}$ ♩ ♩

Mode II $\frac{3}{4}$ ♩ ♩

Mode III $\frac{6}{4}$ ♩. ♩ ♩

In monophonic song Mode III might also be interpreted:

$\frac{2}{2}$ ♩ ♩ ♩

The last three modes, though important in polyphonic music, are not used by most scholars who consider the use of the rhythmic modes valid in the transcription of monophonic song.

Mode IV $\frac{6}{4}$ ♩ ♩ ♩.

Mode V $\frac{6}{4}$ ♩. ♩.

Mode VI $\frac{3}{4}$ ♩ ♩ ♩

rhythmic mode as a means of treating the many two-note groups on unaccented syllables may also be considered. In triple time the basic rhythm of the third mode is $\genfrac{}{}{0pt}{}{6}{8}$ ♩. ♪♪ ; in duple time it is $\genfrac{}{}{0pt}{}{2}{4}$ ♩ ♫ . The patterns of the rhythmic modes are shown in Chart I. Several of the songs which are more melismatic have been transcribed in free rhythm, in which the written notation represents only an approximation of the rhythmic performance. These songs include three of the four *Spruch* melodies – the first, the second, and the fourth – and Minnesongs II and IV.

The forms used by Wizlaw are all based on the *Barform* (A A || B). His favorite type uses all or part of the *Stollen* melody at the end of the *Abgesang*, (A A || B A), and he uses this principle in many ways. Surprisingly enough the poetic and musical forms often do not correspond exactly in the closing repeat of the *Stollen* melody. The most striking case of this sort of treatment is found in the *Ton* of *Sprüche* X and XI, in which the melody is almost exactly repeated at the end, but the line lengths of the texts are not the same as in the *Stollen*, thus making the cadence points fall on new notes in the melody when it is last repeated.

All but three of the minnesongs use some variation of the form A A || B A. One of the songs in this form, Minnesong XIII, is incomplete, but enough of the concluding repeat is present to indicate that the melodic repeat is exact. Four melodies use the *Barform* without any repeat of the earlier melody at the end (A A || B); of these three are minnesongs and one is a *Spruch*. The other *Sprüche* use a form which somewhat resembles the double versicle structure of the *Leich* segment. The basic pattern is A A || B B A, but, as Wizlaw uses it, any of the repeats in the *Abgesang* may be variations rather than literal repetitions. Thus, the *Ton* of *Sprüche* I-IX is A A || B B' A; the *Ton* of *Sprüche* X and XI is A A || B B' A'; and only in *Spruch* XII is the pattern simply A A || B B A. Since the song of disputed authorship at the beginning of the manuscript includes only the two *Stollen* and the very beginning of the *Abgesang*, it is impossible to hazard a guess as to the nature of its complete form.

The scales used in the melodies include both plagal modes, in which the range of the melody lies above and below the final tone, and authentic modes, in which the range of the melody is above the final tone. The range of several of the songs is quite wide, encompassing an octave and a half (the combined range of the plagal and authentic modes with the same final note). Though in most minnesongs Dorian and Lydian are the favorite modes, Wizlaw does not use the Dorian mode at all and uses the Lydian only once, in Minnesong XII. Two songs use the plagal Hypolydian mode. The modes he prefers, however, are Phrygian (Minnesongs I, II, and IV) and Aeolian (Minnesongs V and VII). He also uses Ionian, which is like the modern major scale, and Mixolydian, as well as the plagal modes Hypoionian, Hypoaeolian, and Hypomixolydian. The distinction between the authentic and plagal modes is sometimes blurred by the wide range of some of the songs. The effect of some of the modes is also blurred by the extensive use of the B-flat. In the Hypolydian songs the real effect is like modern F major; in the Mixolydian and Hypomixolydian songs B-flat is used so extensively that the sound is often like modern G minor; and in the Aeolian songs the frequent B-flats give the effect of Phrygian. Thus, Wizlaw's most characteristic tonal atmospheres are actually Phrygian, modern major, and modern natural minor, even though the last two were not recognized by theorists until 1547 in the *Dodecachordon* of Glareanus. The characteristics of the medieval modes are shown in Chart II.

The song of disputed authorship which comes at the beginning of the portion of the manuscript containing Wizlaw's songs and the first two *Spruch* melodies known definitely to be by Wizlaw are all melismatic songs. They have, therefore, been transcribed to be sung in free rhythm, with the text scansion given at the beginning of each line, indicating whether or not the line begins with an *Auftakt* (weak syllable up-beat).

The complete musical form of the incomplete *Spruch* cannot be determined, but its *Stollen* has an interesting pattern with varied repetition of a short middle phrase: A B B' C. The B and B' phrases are short, with the second an abbreviated form of the first. The musical form of the first *Spruch* clearly ascribed to Wizlaw is A A || B B' A. Up-beats are freely added to repeated sections and the melody of the B sections is constructed from the cadential formula which ends the *Stollen*. Much of the song is built around the quasi-chromatic use of B-flat and B-natural, which is indicated in the cadence of the second line of the poem. A more elaborate form of the same cadence comes at the end of the fourth line, the end of the *Stollen*.

The second *Spruch* melody, that was used for *Sprüche* X and XI, is the one whose form differs so greatly from the poetic form. Perhaps the latter was changed in the process of translation from Low German; perhaps the melody was adapted by the scribe who wrote the Wizlaw section of the Jena Manuscript and forced to fit the standard A A || B A pattern, even though the poem may never have followed this metric structure. In any case, the poetic form is the same for both *Sprüche* and the melody fits both equally well.

In contrast to the first two melodies, that of *Spruch* XII is in a very simple style and uses a very restricted range. It has been transcribed in triple meter, using a mixture of the first and second rhythmic modes. In the feminine cadences which close each *Stollen* both the heavy and weak syllables are treated as long notes.

The most complicated melodic ornamentation of all the Wizlaw songs is found in the music of the last *Spruch*. The long opening melisma consists of three neumes which provide an elaborate decoration for the *Auftakt* C, which descends first a third; then, with melodic decoration, a fourth; and finally,

CHART II

The Medieval Modes

Mode   Range   Dominant   Final

I. Dorian

II. Hypodorian

III. Phrygian

IV. Hypophrygian

V. Lydian

VI. Hypolydian

VII. Mixolydian

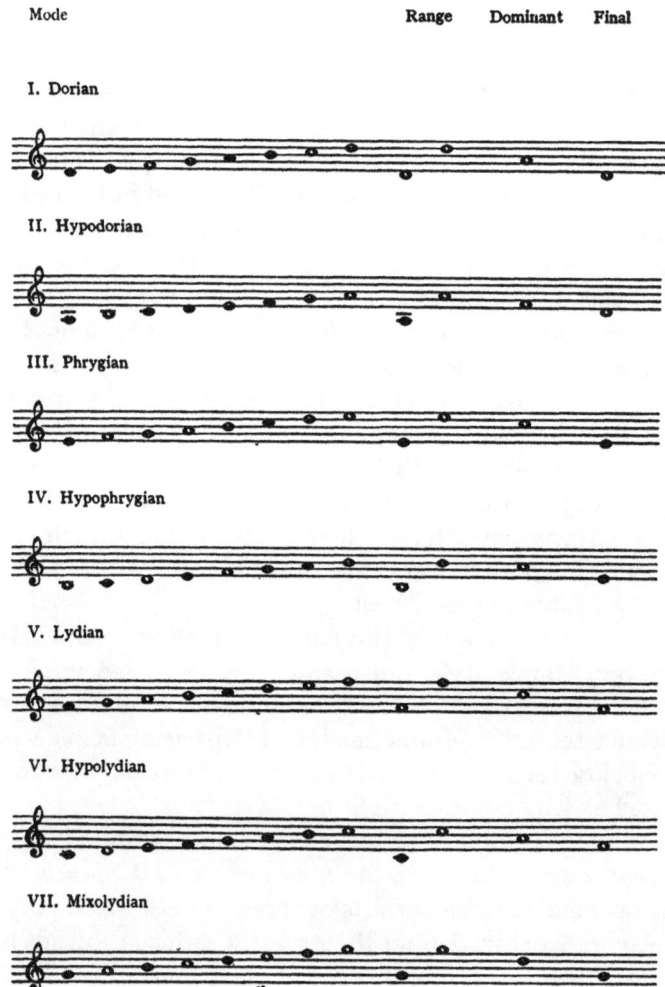

VIII. Hypomixolydian

These last four modes were not recognized by theorists until the Renaissance.

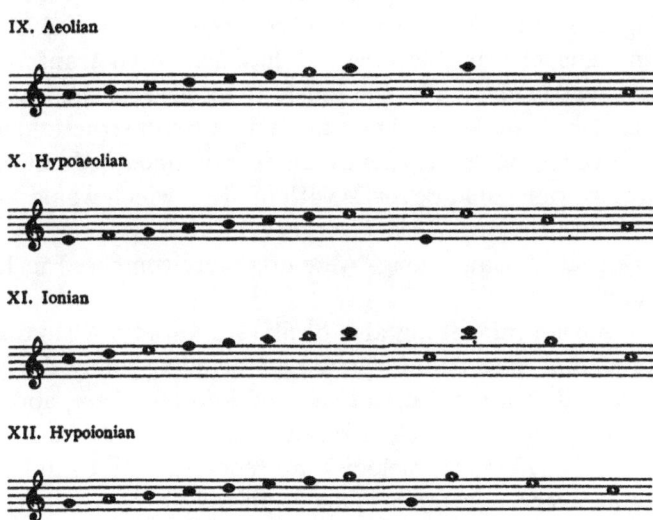

with still more decoration, a fifth, to anticipate the note of the first strong syllable. Elaborate melismas are also added at the end of each line. The ornamentation includes appogiatura-like figures, such as those at the end of the first line; trills; turns; and runs of up to a fifth in range. The range of the whole song is an octave and a fifth, and the upper limits of the range are higher than those of any other song except Minnesong XII. The great elaboration as the poet describes the angels carrying the soul to heaven reminds one of the ecstatic joy expressed in the melismas of the Gregorian *Alleluia* melodies, and gives the song a rapturous quality far beyond the rather conventional expression of the text. The rhythmic symbols used in the transcription are not to be taken in an exact sense, but represent only an approximation of a free rhythmic rendering.

The simple, expressive melody of the first minnesong is one of the loveliest of all minnesongs. The metric structure is rather unusual in its consistent use of a dactyl in the second line of the *Stollen*. Though its first appearance is somewhat ambiguous, it is unmistakable in the second *Stollen* and in the closing line of the *Abgesang*. It has here been transcribed with a metric change in the music to emphasize the shift in the pattern. In Margarete Lang's text reconstruction into Low German, however, this irregularity is smoothed out, and a transcription could be made with her text which would have no metric changes. This fact gives further support to the theory that Wizlaw's songs were originally composed in Low German.

The second minnesong also displays a variety of rhythmic patterns and may be interpreted as including many dactyls. However, they are not used in a regular fashion here, and the transcriber faces a problem rarely found in Wizlaw's songs, namely, that identical melodies are repeated with completely different accent patterns. One is forced to conclude that, whatever patterns may work for other minnesongs, any system such as that of the rhythmic modes which tries to make long notes correspond with strong syllables will certainly not produce satisfactory results with this song. Furthermore, the melodic structure seems to be based on a series of melodic cells which begin with the same pitch succession, though often with reversed accent patterns, and end differently each time. It seems, therefore, that a free and improvisatory manner would be the most suitable for singing this song, and the barlines are given in the transcription only to indicate the pattern of strong beats. The form is quite complicated and the melodic rhyme of the beginning of the first three lines is particularly interesting. The musical pattern of Minnesong II is:

Stollen $\begin{cases} A \\ A' \\ A'' \\ B \end{cases}$

Stollen $\begin{cases} A \\ A' \\ A'' \\ B \end{cases}$

Abgesang $\begin{cases} C \\ C' \text{ (accent shift only)} \\ D \\ D' \text{ (change of cadence melody)} \\ A \\ A' \\ A'' \\ B. \end{cases}$

In no one of the appearances of A-derived phrases after the first one of each *Stollen* is the pattern of accents within the lines the same, even when the pitch succession is the same.

The third minnesong again uses a very wide range of an octave and a half, combining the ranges of the authentic and plagal modes. The climax of the song occurs in the phrase which begins the *Abgesang*. Though the basic pattern is that of a *Barform* with part of the *Stollen* repeated, the place of the repeat does not exactly correspond with the poetic form. The result is that one has almost reached the end of the song before realizing that much of the *Stollen* has been repeated, but with the beginning of the repeat skillfully woven into the fabric of the line. The structure of the song is as follows:

Stollen $\begin{cases} A \\ B \\ C \text{ (condensed combination of A and B)} \end{cases}$

79

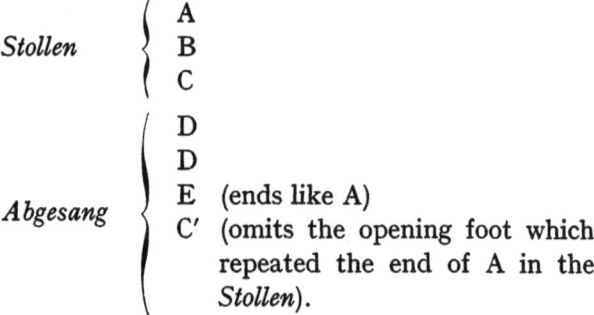

The only melismatic minnesong is the fourth one, which is, unfortunately, incomplete in the manuscript. The form must have been similar to that of the last *Spruch*. The greatest amount of melismatic writing is on the concluding vowel *o* which ends each line of the first stanza, and, since the text mentions the singing of birds, one may assume that this warbling passage was intended as text-painting.

Minnesong V presents a striking contrast with the preceding song. The melody demands a vigorous, regular, and strongly accented performance. Though the poet speaks of the pain of frustrated passion, the dance-like jauntiness of the tune belies the anguish of his words and puts them into the perspective of a charming, and fleeting, game.

The formal pattern of the sixth minnesong represents a new solution to the problem of a repeated musical section that does not correspond to the form of the end of the *Abgesang* of the text. In this song the form is changed by repeating only the first two phrases of the *Stollen* tune and adding a new phrase which repeats the cadence of the second line as a substitute for the two longer phrases which originally concluded the *Stollen*. The structure, therefore, is:

Stollen { A B C D

Stollen { A
B
C
D

Abgesang { E
F
A
B
X (cadence as in B).

In Minnesong VII the *Stollen* is itself made up of repeated phrases, while the *Abgesang* combines new material with fragments from the *Stollen* in a melodic mosaic:

Stollen { A
B
A
B
C

Stollen { A
B
A
B
C

Abgesang { D
E (cadence as in C)
A (includes cadence similar to C)
X (expansion of preceding cadence)

Stollen { A
B
A
B
C.

The melodic form of the *Stollen* is itself a miniature *Barform*.

Although Minnesong VIII is in the Hypoaeolian mode, the distinctive repeated cadence closing the two *Stollen* and the *Abgesang* and used again at the end of the first phrase of the *Abgesang* contains a striking use of the B-flat. Through the pattern C A B-flat A a strongly Phrygian flavor is imparted to the melody. The range of the song is very restricted and strongly emphasizes the descending minor third from C to A. Except for the cadence at the end of the first line of the *Abgesang*, which is borrowed from the *Stollen*, the form is quite conventional (A A || B A).

The metric complexities and involved rhyme scheme of Minnesong IX are well-matched by the melodic ingenuity used in the construction of the tune. The first line ends with the cadence A B-flat C. The second line, which rhymes with the first, exactly reverses this pitch succession in the cadence C B-flat A. The opening word of line three rhymes with the cadence of the preceding line, and the melodic pattern is again reversed, but with a slight change: A B-natural C. The same relationship, of course, is found in the repeat of the *Stollen* melody. The *Abgesang* begins with the pitch which was the highest point of the *Stollen* melody, repeats the same note (G) for three long rhyming syllables and then leaps up exuberantly to a high C, a peak reached in only one other melody by Wizlaw. At the words *bluote, ghuote, suote ich* he begins a sequence of sighing figures which drop down from G to C, leap up again to G on the word *vroyden* (joy), and descend once more in a new pattern to C. He ends the *Abgesang* with another rise to G and a final cadence which uses the same pitches as the cadence of the *Stollen*. No other portion of the *Stollen* is repeated in the *Abgesang*.

In the tenth minnesong there is a clef error, since, as it stands in the manuscript, the song is in the Hypolocrian mode (with the final tone on B), which theoretically is impossible at this period. If, however, the clef is read as an F clef, the song can be considered to be in the Hypophrygian mode. The melody is a fairly conventional *Barform* with no repeat of *Stollen* material in the *Abgesang*.

The melody of the eleventh minnesong is somewhat similar to that of the second, though without any of the accentual complexities of the latter. The *Abgesang* borrows the last half of the *Stollen* melody and then repeats the whole *Stollen* tune:

Stollen	A B C D
Stollen	A B C D
Abgesang	E F C D A B C D.

Though the melody of Minnesong XII is very simple in structure and has a conventional A A || B A pattern, it possesses a grace and purity of style which makes it one of the most appealing of the group. The last song, on the other hand, which also has a conventional A A || B A form (though incomplete in the manuscript), is made up of rather stiff repetitive formulas. Though it is transcribed in duple time, it could be sung equally well in the first mode, which might somewhat enliven its rather stodgy character.

In the performance of all these songs the singer must keep in mind that the original notation was *not* mensural, and that the suggestions of the transcriptions should be interpreted with freedom. This is especially to be remembered in the case of the first two *Spruch* melodies, the last *Spruch*, and Minnesongs II and IV, where a free and flexible rhythm is necessary. In the other songs, the singer should adopt a tempo which will keep the movement flowing and avoid a dragging or stilted style.

If instruments are used in the performance of the songs, they may be added in several ways: they may simply double the singer's line; improvise preludes, postludes or interludes; or perform with the singer a simplified or ornamented version of the melody. The best instruments for use with the songs would be lute, recorder, vielle (or other stringed instruments played with a light, clear sound), and percussion instruments such as small drums, finger cymbals, bells, or a small tambourine.

In the original performance of the minnesongs the singer was free to display his ability by embellishing or varying the tunes. Although the modern performer is no longer trained in the tradition of improvised embellishment, he should keep this creative performance tradition in mind and approach the rhythmic performance and instrumental accompaniment of these songs with an experimental spirit, which, though it will never exactly recapture what the minnesingers did, will bring their songs to life in this century with the freshness and vigor which they had in their own day.

CHAPTER SIX

THE MANUSCRIPT

The extant songs of all the minnesingers appear in nearly fifty manuscripts and fragments of manuscripts, some containing several hundred songs, a few containing only one or two. The oldest of the larger manuscripts, the Old Heidelberg Manuscript, was compiled by four successive scribes during the period from the late thirteenth century to the end of the fourteenth century. The collection includes lyrics by thirty-four minnesingers but has no music notation. The next important collection, which also has no music, is the Weingarten Manuscript. It was prepared at the beginning of the fourteenth century and includes songs by thirty-one minnesingers, twenty-five of whom are pictured in beautiful illustrations. By far the most famous of the collections is the Manesse Manuscript which was prepared during the first half of the fourteenth century. It contains songs by 139 minnesingers and has 138 excellent illustrations. Since the latter show the minnesingers in characteristic situations, they reveal something (in some cases all that is known) of the lives and positions of their subjects. No melodies are included. From the standpoint of the musician the most important manuscript is the Jena Manuscript which was prepared toward the middle of the fourteenth century and contains primarily religious and didactic songs for most of which there is music notation. The songs of thirty composers appear in the Jena Manuscript, the great majority of them from the middle class. Second only to the Jena Manuscript in importance to the musician is the Vienna Manuscript, which contains about the same amount of notation as the former, though from a much smaller number of composers. The manuscript was prepared in the fourteenth century. Two further manuscripts, the Münster Fragment and the Berlin Neidhart Manuscript, are of particular significance to the musicologist because of the antiquity of the music and the importance of the composers represented. The former contains three melodies of Walther von der Vogelweide, the latter fifteen melodies of Neidhart von Reuenthal. Both manuscripts are of fairly recent origin, dating from about the middle of the fifteenth century.

Although the songs of some composers appear in several manuscripts, those of Wizlaw are contained only in the Jena Manuscript. We know nothing definite of the preparation of the collection, but it has been suggested that it was made at the direction of Friedrich the Serious, Landgrave of Thuringia and Margrave of Meissen (1324-1349), that is, soon after Wizlaw's death. Our first certain knowledge of the manuscript, however, comes from a library list of 1434 which indicates that it was then in the chapel of Wittenberg Castle. In 1558 it was given by the House of the Saxon Electors to the newly founded University of Jena where it still remains. The manuscript consists today of 133 folio leaves, but since both the beginning and the end of the manuscript are missing, we cannot know how large it was originally. There are at least nine gaps in the body of the collection, indicating the loss of at least twelve leaves.

Including a *Spruch* of disputed authorship, the works of Wizlaw appear in the manuscript from 72^v to 80^v inclusive; however, four pages have been cut out. Between 74 and 75 a page is missing, but no gap in the text results. Textual losses occurred in the case of the other missing pages: between 72 and 73, between 76 and 77, and between 80 and 81. The controversial *Spruch*, which begins with the words, 'Ihc wil singhen,' appears just before those of Wizlaw in the Jena Manuscript and was written by the same hand as that which recorded his works. It is the only song not commonly ascribed to Wizlaw which was written by this scribe. Nevertheless, until recent, as yet unpublished research by Miss Ermute Uthleb, the *Spruch* has been attributed to Friedrich von Sonnenburg. It and the songs which are generally accepted as being by Wizlaw are in a larger and much more careless hand than those in which the rest of the manuscript was written and the lines for the notation are not red, as with the other compositions, but black. Also the initial letters for the stanzas are red throughout, not alternately blue and red as is otherwise the case, and have no particular adornments. For these reasons, and another yet to be mentioned, it has been suggested that Wizlaw's songs were not originally intended for the collection.

Although composers from all over Germany are represented in the collection, the language in which their poems are presented is Middle German with some High German and some Low German forms. This is also true of Wizlaw's works, but there are particular difficulties in this case which result in some passages being almost unintelligible. The most logical assumption for the confused language is that the scribe was translating from a Low German text and did not know Low German. However, von der Hagen, a nineteenth century minnesong scholar, maintained that Wizlaw wrote in High German. He bases his claim on the fact that the minnesong was a High German phenomenon, that with two exceptions all of the other minnesingers apparently composed in High German, and that, therefore, the minnesongs which Wizlaw would have heard or read would have been in that language. Moreover, it would be only natural for Wizlaw to compose in the traditional language of the minnesong. For his collection of minnesongs von der Hagen, therefore, translated Wizlaw's songs from the Middle German of the manuscript into High German. His contemporary, Ettmüller, however, insisted that Wizlaw had composed in Low German, and published a Low German translation of his works. Ettmüller's reasons for his theory, which has been accepted by most later scholars, are based on both the historical situation and linguistic analysis. There was very little political or commercial connection in the early fourteenth century between the Southern Baltic states and the Empire; Wizlaw probably never journeyed to where High German was spoken; his songs were composed and performed in Rügen where the audiences would not even have understood High German; and the Low German language had attained the stature of an official language, being used together with Latin in official documents. Ettmüller's linguistic evidence is quite convincing, the most important point being that Wizlaw's verse does not rhyme very well in High German, but does in Low German. If it is true, as it seems to be, that Wizlaw composed in Low German, he is probably the only minnesinger to have done so. But he was in a different situation from that of the great majority of the minnesingers of his time. Composition and performance was not his profession and he did not wander from court to court as a professional entertainer who had to compose for the largest possible public. His songs were written for his own enjoyment and that of his friends and he doubtless used the language which they knew best, the Low German of his native Rügen.

In transcribing the texts of the Wizlaw manuscript the following practices have been observed: the scribe's many intentional contractions have been expanded, the vowels which were written above vowels (to indicate *Umlaut*, diphthonal glide or length) have been placed after the primary vowel, and the letters *v* and *u* have been standardized according to modern usage. No attempt has been made to correct the numerous scribal errors.

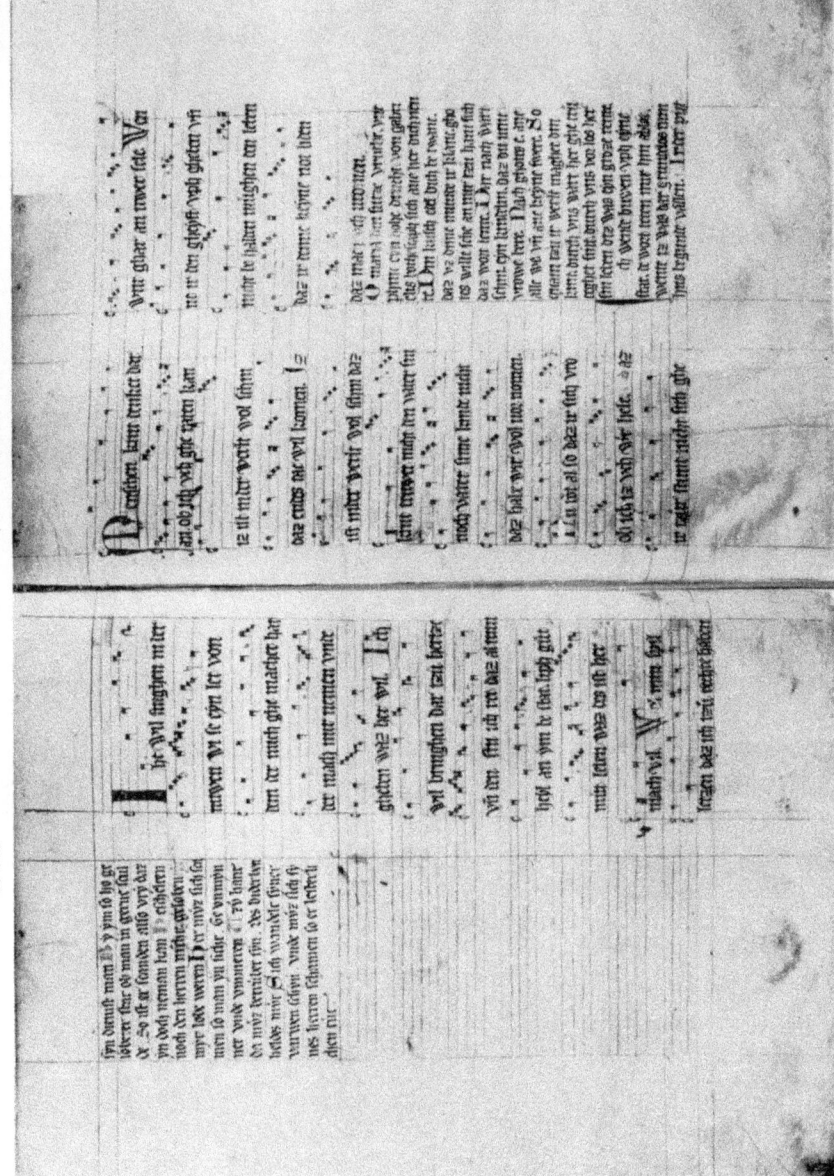

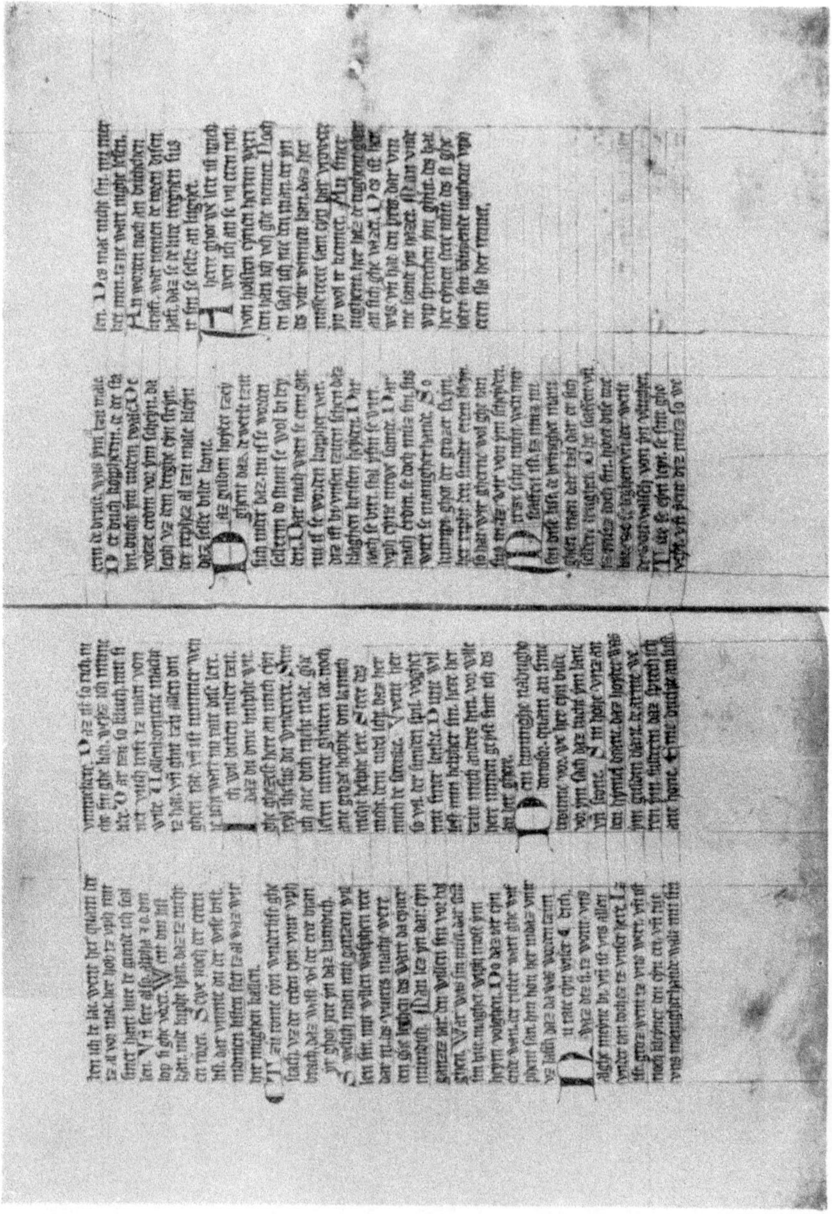

f. 74r

f. 73v

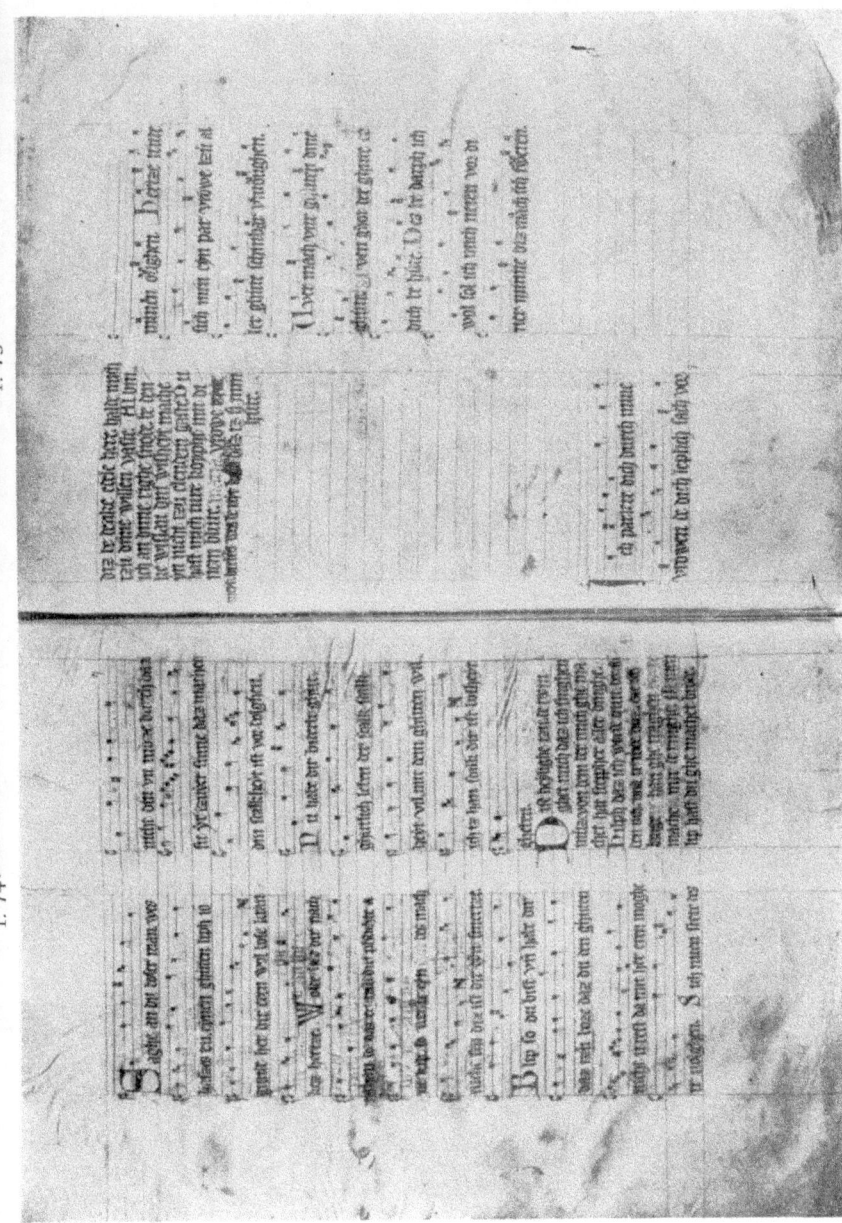

f. 75v

f. 76r

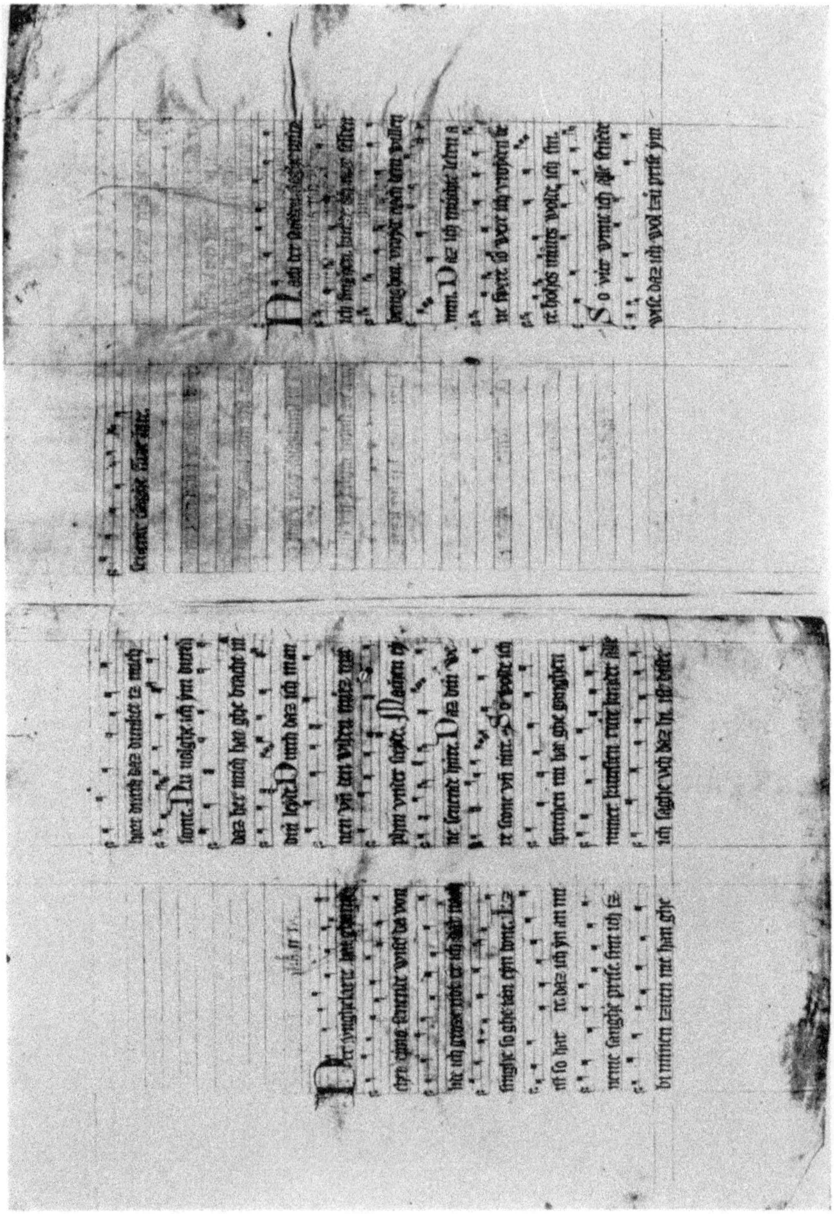

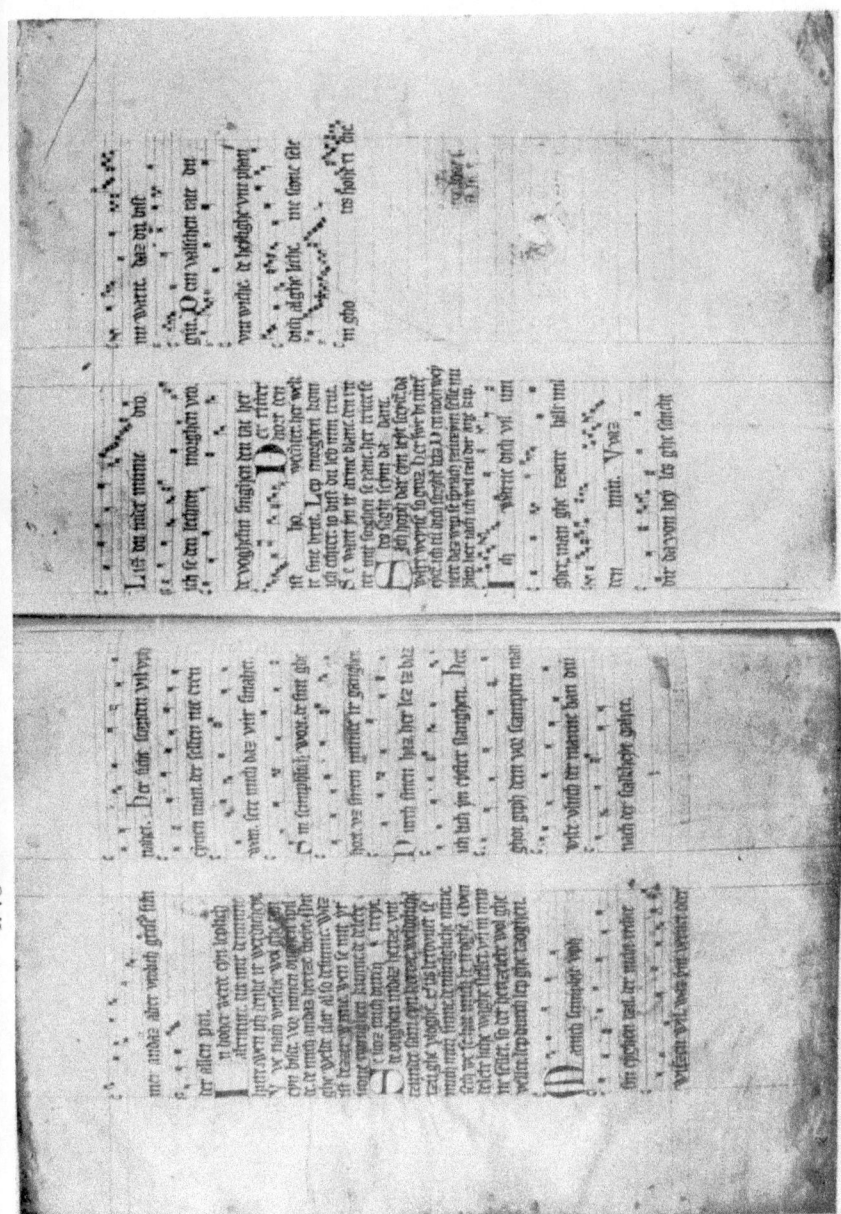

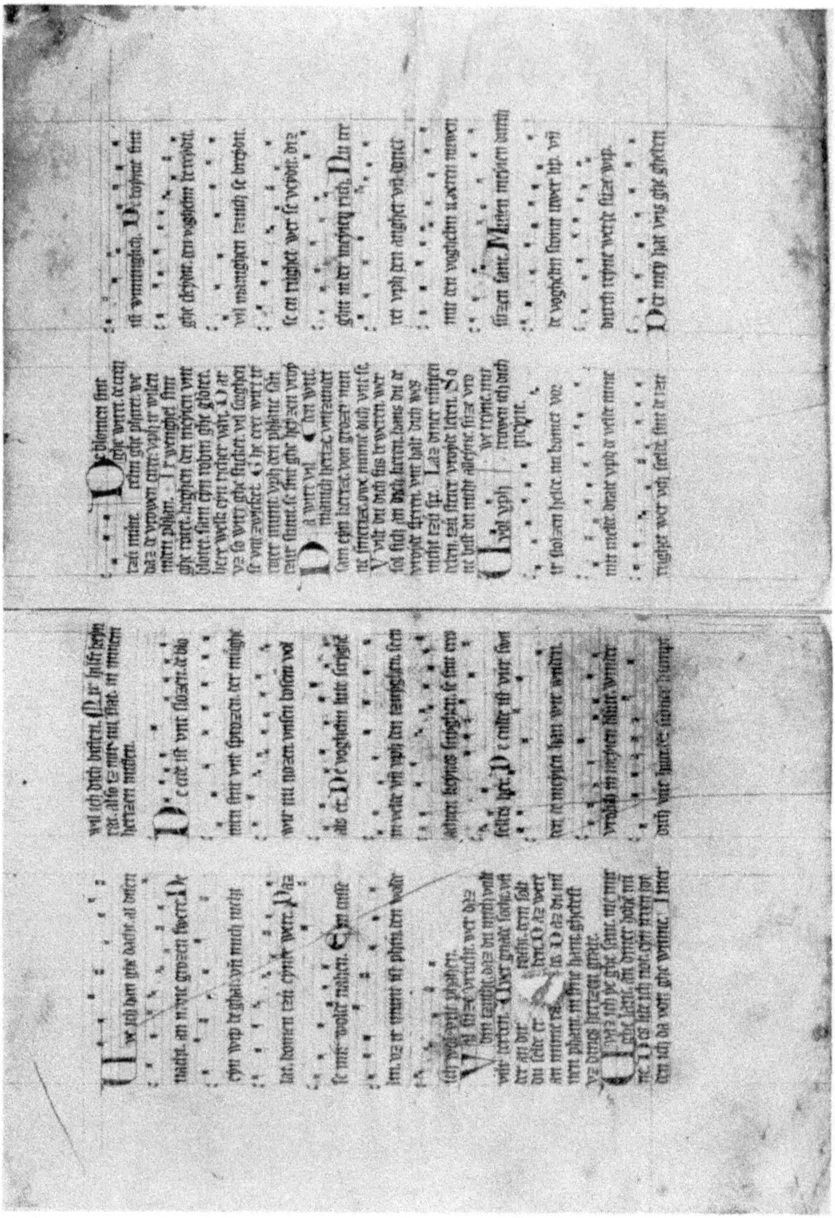

f. 77v

f. 78r

f. 78v f. 79r

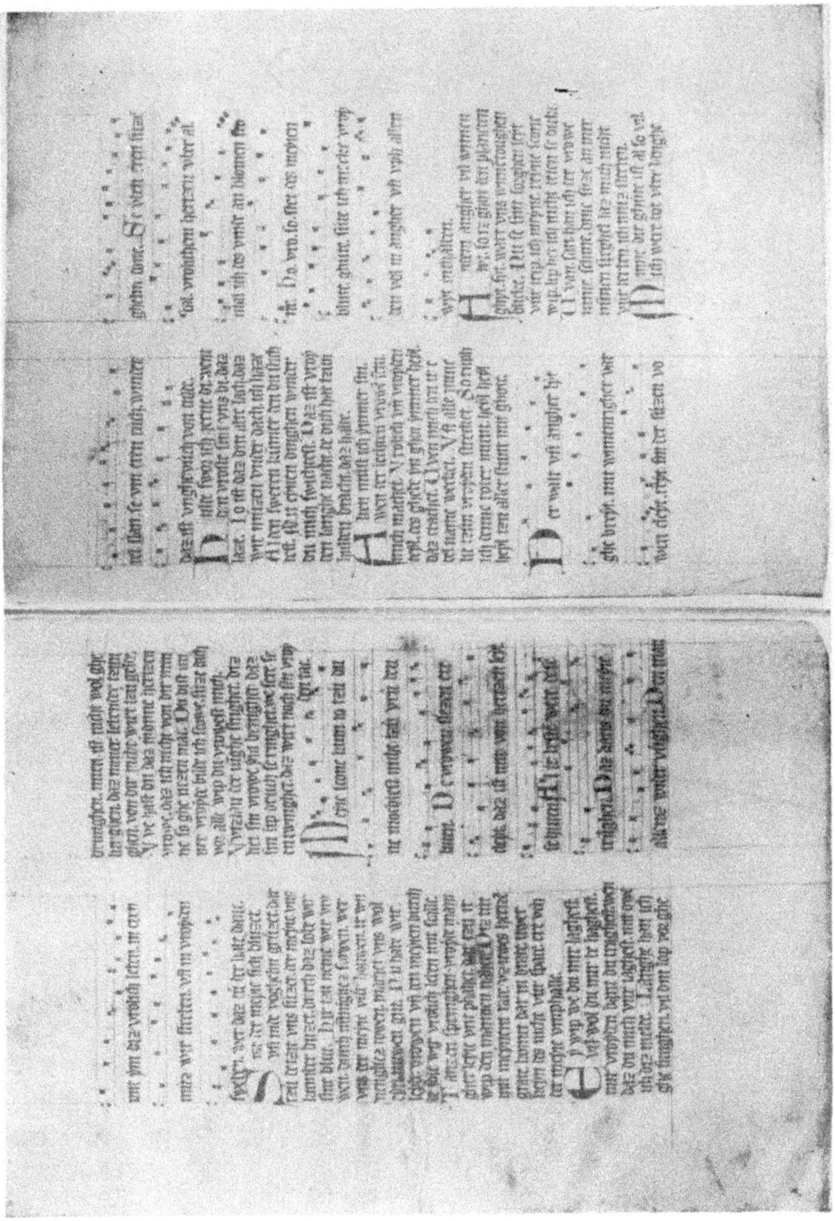

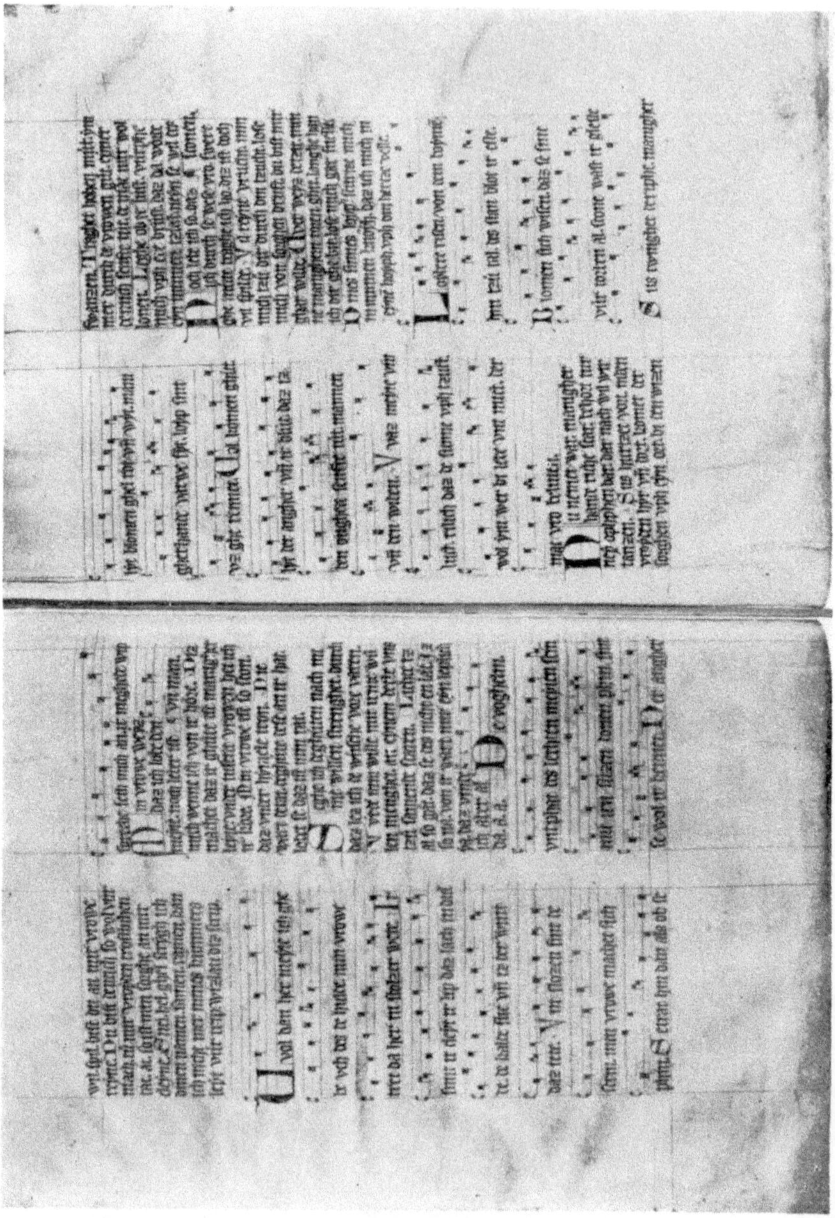

f. 79v f. 80r

f. 80v

f. 81r

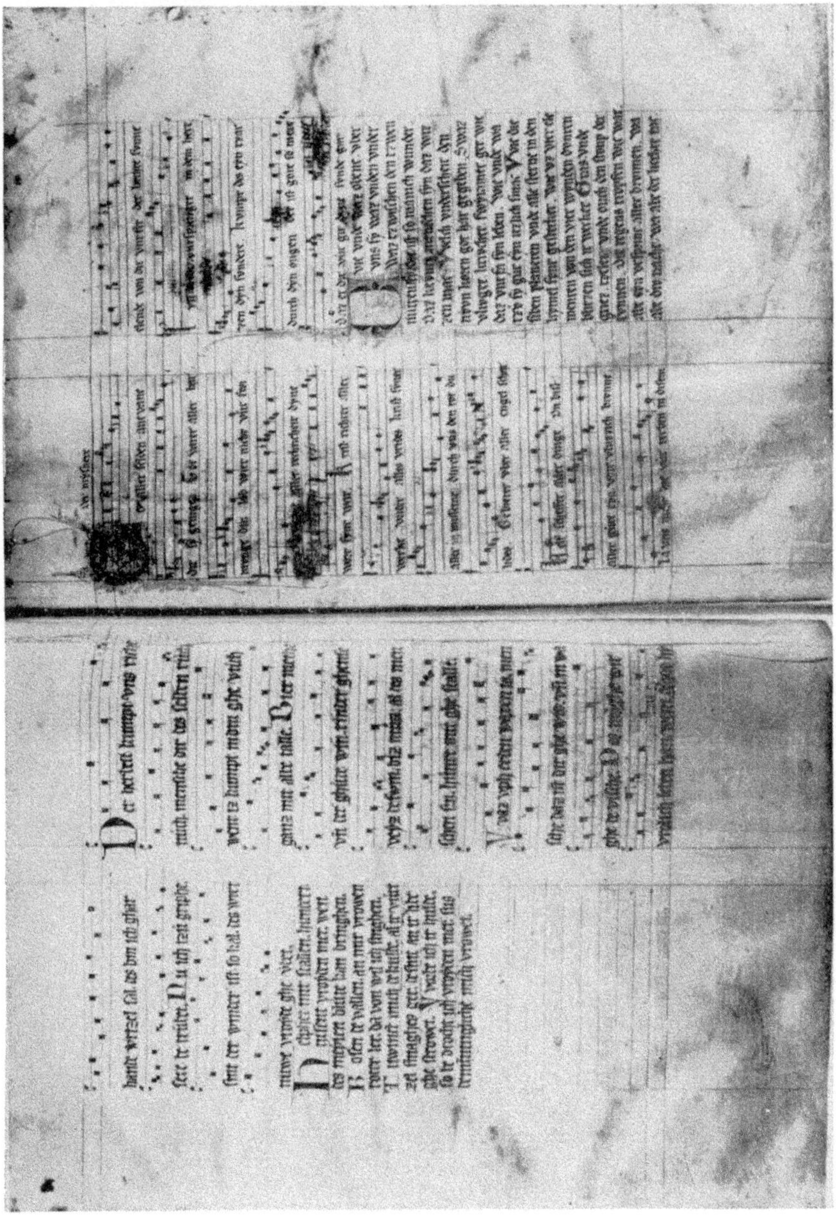

CHAPTER SEVEN

THE TEXTS

IHC WIL SINGHEN

Ihc wil sing-hen in der nu-wen wi- se eyn let

von dem der mich ghe-ma-chet hat der mach mir ne-men

un - de ghe-ben waz her wil.

Ich wil bring-hen dar tzuo hert-ze und den sin ich ret

daz al min heyl an ym be-stat. liph guot, muot le-ben

waz des ist her mach vil.

Wol min spil let-zen daz ich tzuo rech-te ha-ben

I shall sing
to the newest tune a lay
of Him who has created me
who grants to me and takes from me whate'er He will.
I shall bring
to this a grateful heart, and say
whatever gives me joy must be
from Him: my goods, my life; all can He fulfill
and can kill
happiness which now is mine.
. . . .

Sons of men, if you are wise,
you will mark what I advise;
such is now the world it seems
   that judgment day is nearing.
Such is now the world it seems
the child no more his sire esteems,
nor does the father trust his child;
   for that's what we've been hearing.
Let what you do
bring joy to you
when I sing about it.
Preserve your soul
unstained and whole;
you are lost without it.
When at last your spirit leaves you,

when life is done and death receives you,
may you then be saved from sorrow
   and die unfearing.

SPRUCH II

O maria din sutze vrucht.
untphinc eyn hohe drucht.
von gabrielis bothescaph
   sich ave her dich nente.
Din kusch edel dich betwanc.
daz uz dime munde irklanc.
ghotes wille sche an mir
   tzuo hant sich daz wort lente.
Dar nach wart schin.
eyn kindelin.
daz du iuncvrowe bere.
Nach ghotes e.
ane alle we.
und ane keyne swere.
So quam tzuo ir werlt maghet din kint.
durch uns wart her ghecruoceghet sint.
durch uns vorlos her sin leben
   diz was eyn groze rente.

Mary, thy humility
brought a great reward to thee
when the angel Gabriel
   cried, 'Ave, blessed Mary!'
And thy virtue was so great
that thou didst not hesitate,
but replied, 'God's will be done.'
   The angel did not tarry.
Thou, undefiled,

didst bear a child.
God's son, divine and stainless,
appeared on earth;
his human birth
was laborless and painless.
Thus, Virgin, was thy infant born,
whom we did crucify with scorn,
who suffered for our sins and died
   to give us sanctuary.

SPRUCH III

Ich wende buwen uph eyne stat.
de wort teten mir hin ablat.
wente iz was dar grundelos
   min hus begunde vallen.
In der puot- (73ᵛ) ten ich belac.
went her quam der iz al vormac.
her hob iz uph mit siner hant
   lute begunde ich scallen.
Und scre also.
alpha und o.
din lop si ghevouret.
Went din list kan.
in de lupht han.
daz iz nicht enrouret.
Sewe noch der erden list.
darumme du der wise bist.
in dinen listen stet iz al
   waz wir hir muoghen kallen.

I built a house as I had planned,
beside the sea upon the sand,
but underneath was no support
   and soon my house was falling.

It rested in a filthy pool;
He came, who over all doth rule,
and with His hand He raised it up.
   I praised Him, loudly calling,
'Thy grace I know,
Alpha and O,
May Thou be worshipped ever!
Thy mighty arm
protects from harm
that earth and sea can never
destroy the thing which Thou doth prize,
for Thou art powerful and wise.
The words we say are weak indeed,
   but Thine are all-enthralling.'

SPRUCH IV

Tzuo rome eyn wunderlist ghescach.
uz der erden eyn viuor uphbrach.
daz wast wul der erde bran
   yr ghot tete yn daz kuondich.
Swelich man mit ganzen willen sin.
mit vollen wafphen rete darin.
des viuores macht were den gheleghen.
   des wart da eyner muondich.
Man lez yn dar.
eyn ganziz iar.
den willen sin vorbolghen.
War was sin muot.
dar stunt sin huot.
maghet wiph most ym heym volghen.
Do daz iar eyn ende wan.
der ritter wart gewafphent san.
hin houv her in daz viuor uzlasch
   daz da was worden tzuondich.

From Rome a wondrous story came
of how the earth was rent with flame;
The very ground began to burn.
   The people's god then stated:
'If ever armored knight or squire
should spur his steed into the fire,
the flame and smoke would vanish.'
   A knight, it is related,
did volunteer
and for a year
his wishes ruled the city.
Whate'er he sought
to him was brought
and all the maidens pretty.
When finally the year was gone,
he put his sword and armor on
and rode into the fire, and then
   the raging flames abated.

SPRUCH V

Nu rate eyn wiser waz diz si.
iz wont uns alghemeyne bi.
und ist uns allen undertan
   doch ez ist unser here.
Iz ist groz went iz uns wert.
und ist noch kleyner den eyn ert.
und tuot uns manigherhande walt
   mit sin ummekere.
Daz ist so rich.
nicht sin ghelich.
weyz ich imme libe.
Dartzuo so kluch.
mit siner vuoch

trist iz man von wibe.
Vollenkomene macht iz hat
und ghit tzuo allen dinghen rat.
und ist tummer wen ie icht wart
   nu rate dise lere.

Guess what this is, if you're so wise:
It is a thing that all must prize
though it is subject to us all,
   no homage it confesses.
It's large enough our lord to be
and still is smaller than a pea,
but yet it causes us much grief
   and harm with its excesses.
There's nothing which
is quite as rich
in me, that I discover;
it's very smart
but still can part
a maiden from her lover.
It has the power of a king
and gives advice to everything,
but nothing ever was so dumb;
   now let me hear your guesses.

SPRUCH VI

Ich wil biten in der tzit.
daz du dine hulphe wit.
gheghezest here an mich eyn teyl
   ihesus du wunderere.
Sint ich ane dich nicht mac.
gheleben nimer ghuoten tac.
noch ane groze helphe din
   la mich nicht helphe lere.

Stete des nicht.
dem tubel icht.
daz her mich bescrenke.
Went her so vil.
der sunden spil.
voughet mit siner lenke.
Dune willest min helpher sin.
here her tzuot mich anders hin.
vorvulle here minen geyst
    sint ich des an dir ghere.

I would pray Thee, Lord, that Thou
grant me Thy assistance now
from ample treasures of Thy grace,
    O Ruler of creation.
For without Thee as my stay
I could have no happy day
and I shall always need Thy help
    to keep me from temptation.
On Thee I call,
let me not fall
into the devil's power,
for he prepares
deceitful snares
for them he would devour.
Lord, shouldst Thou not rescue me,
I'd be drawn away from Thee.
Renew, O Lord, my weary soul;
    hear this my supplication.

SPRUCH VII

Dem kuninghe nabughodonosor.
quam an sime troume vor.

we her eyn bilde vor ym sach
    daz tucht ym lanc und scone.
Sin hoehe unz an den hymel dranc.
daz hoybet was ym guldin blanc.
de arme weren ym sulberin
    daz sprech ich ane hone.
Eme duchte an lust (74 r)
erin de brust.
was ym al tzuo male.
Der buch koeppherin.
de dee stalin.
ducht ym in dem twale.
De voutze erdin vor ym scheyn.
da leph uz dem berghe eyn steyn.
der reph ez al tzuo male kleyn
    daz selbe bilde kone.

Daz guldin hoybet tzeyghent daz.
de werlt tzut sich nider baz.
nu is se worden selberin
    do stunt se wol bi beyden.
Darnach wart se erin gar.
nu ist se worden koppher var.
diz ist bi unsen tziten schen
    daz klaghen kristen heyden.
Darnach se birt.
stal ysin se wirt.
uph eyne nuwe scande.
Darnach erdin.
se doch muoz sin.
sus wirt se manigherhande.
So kumpt ghot der grozer steyn.
her ripht den sunder erdin kleyn.
so hat wir gherne wol ghetan
    sus muoz wir von ym scheyden.

To Nebuchadnezzar, Lord Supreme
of Babylon, within a dream
the likeness of a man appeared,
   a fair and mighty wonder.
Against the heavens it could hold
a massive head of shiny gold,
of gleaming silver were its arms;
   the monarch saw thereunder–
I do not jest–
a brazen breast,
a belly made of copper,
and iron thighs
of giant size,
but, what seemed hardly proper,
below were feet of common clay.
A stone swept down the mountain gray
and struck the image with such force
   each part was torn asunder.

The golden head that towered high
recalls a golden age gone by,
and then a silver epoch came;
   in both the earth has thriven.
To brass the world was changed anew,
and then acquired a copper hue;
this happened in our times, and pain
   to all mankind was given.
The modern stage,
an iron age,
beneath its shame has ground us,
and then one day
the earth was clay,
we see it all around us.
Soon God, the mighty stone, will greet
the ones who have no earthen feet,
but those who practice evil deeds
   from God shall then be driven.

SPRUCH VIII

Mir geschit nicht wen mir scaffen ist.
iz muoz nu sin dise list.
de bringhet manighen man dartzuo.
    dar er sich selben trughet.
Ghescaffen und iz muoz doch sin.
horet dise torelin
we se leghen und der werlt
    de wort valsch von yn vlughet.
Tuot se eyn leyt.
se sint gheveyt.
und yent diz muoz so wezen.
Des mac nicht sin.
nu merket min.
iz ne wart ni ghelesen.
An worten noch an buochchen kraft.
war nemen de toren disen haft.
daz se de lute treghen sus
    ir sin se selbe an lughet.

'Whate'er befalls me, small or great,
was meant to be and is my fate.'
This saying causes many men
    to reach a false conclusion.
'Twas meant to be' and 'Fate' are fools
and those who hear them are their tools,
but, though they spread throughout the world
    much sorrow and confusion,
they can't be harmed,
their lives are charmed,
for all they take the credit.
This should not be,
give ear to me;
no one has ever read it

in any book, of this I'm sure.
How can these fools be so secure
when they deceive the people thus
   with lies and self-delusion?

SPRUCH IX

A herre ghot we lebe ist mich.
wen ich an se vil eren rich.
von holsten eynen herren wert
   den han ich uch ghenennet.
Noch ensach ich nie den man.
der yn des vuorwinnen kan.
daz her missetrete sam eyn har
   vrow ere yn wol irkennt.
An siner iunghent.
her hatz de tughent
ghar an sich ghevazet.
Des ist her wis.
und hat den pris.
darumme scande yn hazet.
Man unde wip sprechen ym ghuot.
des hat her eynen stete muot.
des si ghelobet sin bluoyende iughent
   uph eren sla her rennet.

Dear God, how great is my delight
when I behold this noble knight,
the worthy Lord of Holstein whom
   I often have commended.
Never have I seen a man
win him to a deed or plan
that was evil by a hair;
   Dame Honor has he defended.

Although a youth
he sought the truth
and virtue of the sages,
now he is wise
and has this prize;
see how Dishonor rages.
Men and women both agree
in praises of his constancy.
We laud the blooming youth of him
who Honor's path ascended.

SPRUCH X

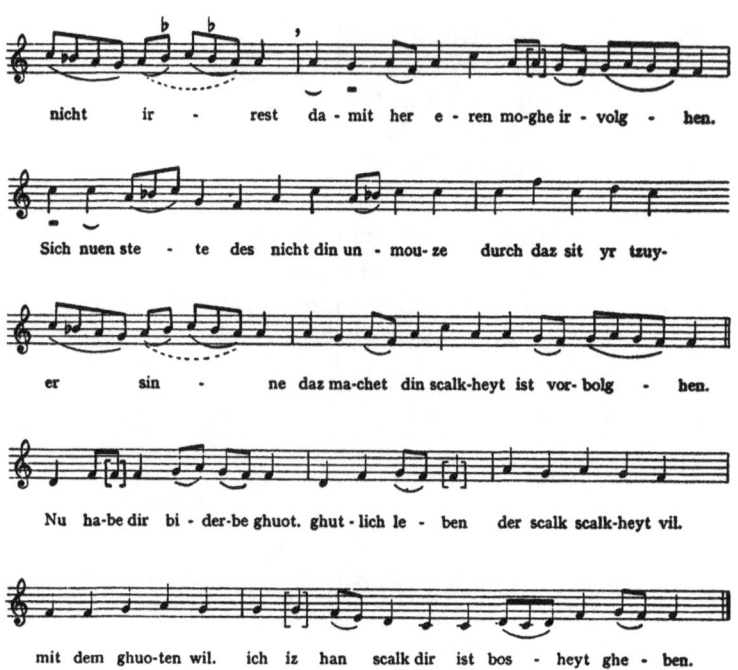

Wicked man, Oh why
must you so hate
him who's good and true,
who'd envy you no wealth or fame
   though your heart is vicious?
If he were to try
to reach a state
of harmony with you,
we both know well, he'd not succeed
   you are too suspicious.
Stay as you are, and may you some day rue it,
but hurt not him who is kindly,
   that wealth and honor be his wages.
Still, your jealousy cannot undo it.

You alone have caused the quarrel
   with knavery and evil rages.
Good sir, I wish you the good life for which
                                    you've striven,
and you, knave, knavery.
I shall always be
with the good, to you, knave, evil is given.

SPRUCH XI

Dise heylighe tzit
de twinghet mich
daz ich singhen muoz.
von dem der mich ghemachet hat
   sceppher aller dinghe.
Hilph daz ich werde quit.
der sunden rich.
und ir werde buoz.
de ich lange han ghetragen.
   mache mir de ringhe.
Minen lip hast du ghemachet brode. (75^r)
diz bedenke edele here.
   halde mich tzuo dime willen vaste.
Al bin ich an dime righe snode.
bedenke wislav din wisheyt
   mache yn nicht tzuo elendem gaste.
Du hast mich ture koypht mit dinem bluote.
vrowe reyne meyt
bittens wis bereyt
kegen din kint daz iz si min houte.

This most holy day
has prompted me
to sing a grateful song

of Him who made me and all things.
    Ruler and Creator,
free me from the sway
of sin's decree;
may I atone the wrong
which I have done and now repent.
    Make my virtue greater!
Thou hast made this body so unstable,
remember this, my noble Master,
    keep my will to Thine subjected.
Though I can't be worthy of Thy table,
think of Wizlaw in Thy wisdom,
    let him never be rejected;
with Thy blood Thou purchased my salvation.
Mary, holy maid,
ask thy Son for aid,
may he always guard me from temptation.

SPRUCH XII

Ma - nich scim - phit uph sin ey - ghen tzil. der nicht rech - te wis - zen wil. waz ym ver - net o - der na - het. Her sicht scan - den vil uph ey - nen man. der sel - ben nie e - ren wan. se - re mich daz vuor - sma - het. Sin

Many a man rejects his future prize
when he will not recognize
virtue which is near him.
Though he merits no esteem or fame,
he besmirches each good name;
Oh, that I need fear him!
His evil word
is often heard
and always is malicious
with bitter hate
for low and great;
no serpent is so vicious.
Bestow upon this villain, Lord,
scorn of men as his reward
and may the women jeer him.

77ʳ   SPRUCH XIII

Ich   war - ne dich vil
Waz   dir da- von hey-

iung - her   man ghe - tzar - te   halt
lez   ghe - schicht   nu war - te.   daz

mil - den   muot.
du   bist   guot.

Dem val-schen ra - te du unt-wi - che. de hey-lighe unt-phan dich

al ghe - li - che.   Di - ne sco - ne

se-le in gho -   tes

ho - he   ri -   che.

The small notes are the grouping for the second *Stollen*.

* The grouping in the manuscript may also be interpreted as:

wi - che.de heylighe unt-phan

116

Give heed, O gentle youth, for I must warn you:
be good and kind,
and keep, however fortune may adorn you,
a noble mind.
Of evil counselors may you be wary
and may at last the holy angels carry
your lovely soul to God's fair sanctuary.

* These groups of three may also be performed with the rhythm:

With my faithfulness would I adorn thee,
since my eyes first saw thee in thy beauty.
Love, be mine, and never let me mourn thee,
thou paragon of virtue and of duty.
Oh none can merit thy affection
but God who grants thee His protection;
this I too must have or soon must perish
of love for thee whom I would hold and cherish.

MINNESONG II

Der un- ghe - lar- te hat ghe-ma- chet ey- ne se - nen- de wi - se da- von lide ich gro- ze not eer ich dar-nach sin-ghe so ghe-taan eyn do- ne. Iz ist so har-te. daz ich yn an mi- ne- me san - ghe pri-se. sint ich iz bi mi- nen tzi- ten nie han ghe- hort durch daz dun-ket iz mich sco - ne. Nu volghe ich ym durch daz her mich hat ghe - bracht in diuo ley- de. Durch daz ich man - nen

The Unlearned Bard
composed a melody in mournful phrases.
I shall suffer painfully
    ere I shall learn to sing so sweet an air.
It is so hard
that in this song I offer him my praises;
though I never in my life
    have heard such music, still I find it fair.
Now I compose as he who brought me to this
    sad position
of showing people how to be a poet and
    musician,
how a minnesong is fashioned
that is lovely and impassioned.

Now I have shown to you the art my magic
wand disperses;
children all, I now can say that here's the
tender music to my plaintive verses.

In hoher werde eyn leplich abentuore.
tuot mir de minne huore.
wen ich denke ir werdicheyt.
We nach wunsche wol ghetan eyn bilde.
vor minen oughen spilde.
de mich an daz hertze sneyt.
Mit ghewelte clar also de sunne.
Waz ist bezzer wunne.
wen se mit yr scone twinghen kunne.
de de lebe treyt.

Se scoz mich durch de oughen in das hertze.
unttzundet sam eyn kertze.
weldilichen tzuo ghevloghen.
Sus berouvet se mich min sinne.
de minningliche minne.
seth we se hat mich betroghen.
Wen de lebeliche waghe stellet.
und in minne sellet.
so der hertzelebe wol ghevellet.
lep durch lep ghetzogen.

Now a lover's plaintive song I sing me.
If only it might bring me
all the joys for which I pine.
Could I live without the cares that sadden,
my songs your heart would gladden;
Joyful spirits would be mine.
Never more would I then sing of sorrow,
but my songs would borrow
happiness for every new tomorrow
as my days decline.

A wondrous sight, a magic charm unfolding,
Love made for my beholding.
When I reflect upon such art

a thing of beauty, only seen by lovers,
before my vision hovers
and pains of rapture pierce my heart.
She has splendor which the sun would treasure;
what gives greater pleasure
than the grace which Love in bounteous measure
did to her impart?

Love's dart went through my eyes and found
and like a flying spark   [its mark,
kindled fires which still are burning
in my heart and rob me of my senses.
Thus lovely Love commences
by deceiving all our learning;
in her scales she weighs and makes selections,
fixes our affections,
ardently then under her directions
love for love is yearning.

MINNESONG IV

* In the manuscript 'dro' does not appear until the last note of the phrase. Since, however, the other melismas are placed to take advantage of the melodious quality of the vowel 'o', the syllable 'dro' has been moved back to an earlier position in the phrase.

Der ritter hort den wechter.
her wekte sine brut.
Lep morghen kom ich echter.
io bist du leb min trut.
Se want yn ir arme blanc.
den ritter mit sorghen se ranc.
her trute se des saght se ym da danc.

Sich hoph dar eyn leyt sceyden.
da wart weynen so grouz.
Her swor bi tuuren eyden.
ich tuo dich sorghen bouz.
Dennoch weynete daz wip.
se sprach tzuo tzym selle nu blip.
her iach ich wil tzuo dir ane kip.

*The morning breeze was sweeping
the mist from the castle wall,
the lovers still were sleeping;
then came the watchman's call:**
'Lovers who together lie,
it lightens in the eastern sky,
the birds all greet the morn: day is nigh.'

This caused the knight to sorrow,
he woke the lady pale:
'My love, I'll come tomorrow—
my darling – without fail.'
She threw her arms around the knight
in great distress and held him tight
but he caressed her till her heart was light.

In deepest grief they parted,
the lady was in tears.

* reconstructed

He swore before he started
that she need have no fears.
But all his efforts were in vain,
she cried to him, 'My love, remain!'
He said, 'I'll soon come back again.'

77ᵛ MINNESONG V

We ich han ghe - dacht al di - sen nacht. an mi - ne gro - zen swe - re. De eyn wip be - ghat. und mich nicht lat. ko - men tzuo ey - ner we - re. Daz se mir wol - de na - hen. Eyn cus-se - lin. uz ir munt ist phin. den wolde ich wol unt - pha - hen.

The strongly marked rhythm of the text suggests a vigorous and sharply defined musical rhythm. The transcription above uses duple meter. If triple modal rhythms are applied various solutions suggest themselves:

First mode

* No clef sign appears in the manuscript until the second line of the song.

Second mode (based on the predominance of neumes on weak syllables)

Third mode (triple interpretation of the short units).

This version is not likely to be more than purely speculative; even if the third mode might be valid, it could equally have been performed with duple units.

Vil suoze vrucht.
wer daz din tzucht.
daz du mich wult vuorterben.
Wer gnade socht.
und der an dir rocht.
dem solt du selde erben.
Daz were an mime rate.
Daz du minnen phant.
in sine hant.
ghebest uz dines hertzen grate.

Waz ich ye ghesanc.
nie mir ghelanc.
an diner hohen minne.
Des lide ich not.
eyn irren tot
den ich da von ghewinne.
Imer wil ich dich bitten.
Mir hilft keyn rat.
Also iz mir nu stat.
in minem hertzen mitten.

I weighed my plight
throughout the night
and my most sad ambition,
which a woman wrought
who had no thought
to bring it to fruition.
I hoped to see and greet her.
A little kiss
from her lips is bliss,
I know of nothing sweeter.

For shame, my sweet,
are you discreet,
that you should want to harm him
who love would find
and thinks you kind?
Why don't you try to charm him?
I counsel you to render
a token of
your faithful love
as proof your heart is tender.

The songs I sing
can never bring
to me your true affection.

I suffer pain
and only gain
my death with your rejection.
But still my prayers continue.
We cannot part,
my foolish heart
must ever strive to win you.

MINNESONG VI

De er-de ist unt-slo-zen. de blo-men sint unt-spro-zen. der muo-ghe wir nu no-zen. un-sen bo-sem vol als er. De vo-ghe-lin lu-te scry-ghen. in vel-de und uph den tzuy-ghen. seen ach-ten key-nes sny-ghen. se sint e-res sel-bes heer. De cul-de ist vuor-swun-den de mey-ien han wir vun-den. vro-lich in mey-ien bluo-te. win-der dich vuor-huo-te. der sum-mer kumpt tzuo muo-te.

* The manuscript has

De blomen sint ghewiret.
de crencelin ghephiret.
we daz de vrowen ciret.
uph ir wilen in den phlan.
Ir wenghel sint gheroutet.
keghen den meyien untbloutet.
sam eyn robin ghegloutet.
here welk eyn richer vaan.
Daruz so wirt ghesticket.
vil sorghen se untzwicket.
Gheeret wirt ir roter mund.
uph den phlane saan tzuor stunt.
se sind gheheyzen vroyden wunt.

Da wirt vil manich hertze.
untzundet sam eyn kertze.
von grozer minne smertze.
owe minne dich untse.
Wilt du dich sus beweren.
wer sol sich an dich keren.
kans du de vroyde speren.
unthalt dich wes nicht tzuo spe.
Laz diner minnen deben.
tzuo steter vroyde leben.
So ne bist du nicht alleyne.
suoze vrowe reyne.
mit truwen ich dich meyne.

The fields no more are bare,
the flowers are everywhere,
we go to join them there
in haste with spirits high.
The birds sing noisily
from every bush and tree,
of ice and snow now free,

they're lords of earth and sky.
The woods have lost their chill,
in leafy groves we thrill
with all the joys of May.
Winter, keep away!
The summer has come to stay.

To wreaths the flowers are wound,
with golden thread are bound.
'In blooms so richly gowned,
come, ladies, to the field.'
Their cheeks are all aglow,
like rubies on the snow,
the spring has made them so.
What cloth this scene would yield
if woven on a loom!
They all are free of gloom,
red lips will get their due
upon the green anew;
their pleasures surely won't be few.

There many a heart in vain
is kindled and is slain
by love's consuming pain.
Beware, Oh Love, beware!
If thou show no concern,
who then to thee will turn?
Joy shouldst thou never spurn.
Be not so proud, take care
to let thy loyal knight
partake of love's delight
and thou shalt never be,
sweet lady, far from me.
This is my pledge to thee.

* Though the syllable in parenthesis is present in the manuscript, it is a light syllable which may be omitted by the singer, as indicated by the absence of a note for it in the music.

und in vroy-den swe-ben. wer daz tuo der ha-be danc.

Sint der meyie sich bluozet.
und in de voghelin gruozet.
dartzuo de tzit uns suozet.
der meyie uns kumber buozet.
durch daz lobe wir sine bluot.
Hirtzuo neme wir vrowen.
durch minningliez scowen.
wer uns der meyie vuorhouwen.
ir wunnengliez towen.
machet uns wol eyn nuwen guot.
Nu habe wir beyde vrowen und den meyien
durch de sole wir vrolich leben mit scalle.
Tanzen springhen. vroyde manigherleyie
untphahet.
dartzuo ir wip den mannen nahet.
Diz tuot mit meynem rate.
uz uwes hertzen grate.
komet dar in drate.
uwer keyn des nicht vuorspate.
ere uch der meyie untphalle.

Ey wip. we du mir laghest.
vil wol du mir behaghest.
mir vroyden band du traghest.
wen daz du mich vuoriaghest.
mit owe ich diz melde.
Langhe han ich ghesungen.
vil din lop vorghedrunghen.
mirn ist nicht wol ghelungen
daz miner lebender tzunghen.

von dir nicht wird tzuo gelde.
We hast du daz in dime hertzen vrowe.
daz ich nicht von dir minne so ghenezen mac.
Du bist miner vroyde bilde ich scowe.
suoze dich
vor alle wip du vrowest mich.
Wizlav de iunge singhet.
diz liet sin vrowe ym bringhet
daz sin lip druch se ringhet.
we sere se en twinghet.
daz wirt noch sin vroyden tac.

Ye youths in fancy feather,
come, let us go together
to fields of blooming heather,
for wondrous is the weather,
and hear him not who scolds.
Their springtime splendor wearing,
with branches outward flaring,
the trees are now preparing
for songbirds, homeward faring,
the charm of May unfolds.
Then hasten to the fields and sing along
with the birds their sweetest melody,
and with the May win beauty from the song
for your lives,
and from tender, loving wives.
The May to us has given
a life of sorrows shriven;
we gain, by honor driven,
the joy for which we've striven.
Our thanks, Oh May, to thee.

The May has come in splendor,
the birds a welcome render,

and breezes, soft and tender,
mark winter's full surrender;
May's beauty now we sing.
Our song of praise embraces
also the ladies' graces;
if May were dead, their faces
and lovely gowns and laces
would make another spring.
But now we have both ladies and the Maytime,
May shall bring us joy and naught shall
                                    grieve us
while we sing and dance through night and
                                    daytime
once again.
Therefore, ladies, join the men!
My wise command obeying,
do what your heart is saying,
come now, without delaying,
to where the music's playing,
before the May shall leave us.

Woman, how you torment me,
when you could so content me
and such delights present me,
but no, away you sent me –
alas, that I must tell it.
How oft your lover raises
his voice to sing your praises
in sweetest notes and phrases,
but, though his passion blazes,
you give him naught to quell it.
What's that within your heart I cannot capture,
that will not let you give your love to me?
You are my shrine of bliss, my dream of rapture;
you, my sweet,

alone can make my joy complete.
Wizlaw, the Younger, is singing
this song. His lady is bringing
him sorrow – bitter and stinging.
But hope is ever springing:
how glad that day will be!

78ᵛ MINNESONG VIII

Mey-ie sco-ne kum io tzuo du-ne moch-test
nicht tzuo vruo den lu-ten. De vro-wen sle-zen e-re
cleyt. daz ist mir von her-tzen leyt. se hu-ten.
Al ir bes-ten we-te de se truo-ghen. Daz kans du
mey-ie al-lenz wi-der vuo-ghen. Den man-tel slan se um
e-ren tuoch. win-der daz ist un-ghe-vuoch von cul-de.

79ʳ

* The manuscript has:

134

Hulde swour ich gerne di.
went din vroste sint uns bi.
daz laze.
Io ist daz din alte lach.
daz wir muozen under dach.
ich haze
Al den sweren kummer den du stichtest.
Mit eynen dinghen winder du mich swichtest.
Daz ist vroyden langhe nacht.
de dich hat tzuon hulden bracht.
daz halte.

Alten muost ich ymmer sin.
wen der lechten vrowe scin.
mich machet.
Vrolich und vroyden teyl.
des ghebe yn ghot ymmer heyl.
daz machet.
Wen mich den ir edel name wecket.
Und alle mine lit tzuon vroyden strecket.
So ruoph ich denne roter mund.
heyl heyl heyl tzu aller stunt
mit ghote.

Come to us, delightful May,
long have you remained away,
asleep.
The women wear such dreary clothes,
this is chief among my woes.
They keep
all their pretty dresses from the weather,
but you, fair May, can change this altogether.
They're hidden by the coats they wear
(Winter, this is most unfair)
from cold.

Hold, O Winter, frosts that chill
and I'll be your vassal still.
Forbear!
It's a fault you cannot hide,
making us remain inside.
I share
all the heavy trials that you measure,
but I am silenced by a single pleasure.
It's the long and happy nights
with their amorous delights
so dear.

Here I stay and shall not go,
for my lady's winsome glow
makes me
happy as a blissful boy.
God, take not away this joy,
I beg Thee.
When she gently calls and I awaken
my every member then with joy is shaken
and I exclaim: 'Oh rosy lips,
how my heart with rapture skips!
God bless you.'

MINNESONG IX

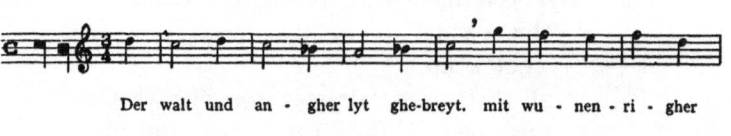

Der walt und an-gher lyt ghe-breyt. mit wu-nen-ri-gher

var-wen cleyt.   reyt   sin der suo-zen voghe-lin do-

An dem angher vil wunnen lyt.
so iz ghot den planeten ghyt.
syt. wart uns wunnentoughen blicke.
Nu se sint sorghen leyt vuortrip.
ich meyne. reyne scone wip.
lip het ich nicht teten se dicke.
Wan. san. han ich der vrowe mine.
schine. dine
suoze an mir minnen speghel laz micht nicht
vuorterben.
ich muoz sterben.

Minne dir ghuote ist al so vil
ich were tot uober langhe (79ᵛ) wil.

spil bist du an mir vrowe reyne.
Du bist dem ich so wol vuormach.
tuo mir vroyden trostlichen tac.
ac. so ist min sorghe an mir cleyne.
Snel. hel. ghel scrygh ich dinen namen.
samen. ramen.
kan ich nicht mer mines kummers leyt vuortrip.
witzlav diz scrip.

The fields and forests, far and near,
in brightly colored dress appear.
Hear the sweet notes from leafy bowers,
the birds are singing a pretty air
with happy spirits everywhere.
Fair is the sight of trees and flowers,
clear, dear, sincere are the Maytime's faces.
Graces, places
of charm I see with joy o'er hills and meadows
far extending.   [wending,

The wonders of the fields in May
are fair as on creation's day.
They can't compare with a new creation,
that drives away each pain and sigh,
a lovely lady, sweet and shy.
I see in her my true salvation.
sight, might, delight, all on me bestowing.
Glowing, showing
kindness to me, Oh darling, my love you must
else I shall perish.   [cherish,

Oh Love, your bounty is so great
that I could die from this joyful state.
Fate has made you my well of gladness
and I am wholly in your power:

grant me many a happy hour,
shower with blessings, banish sadness.
Your name and fame I proclaim, knowing I
shall never,
ever endeavor
to part from that which frees from care and
brings me bliss.
Wizlaw, sing this!

MINNESONG X

There is an apparent error in the clef for this song. If an F clef were substituted for the C clef of the manuscript, the result would be:

Min vrowe weyz daz ich lobe den meyie.
no leber ist mich wenne ich von ir houre.
Diz machet daz ir ghuote ist manigherleyie.
Under tusent vrowen het ich ir koure.
Min vrowe ist so scon.
daz under hymele tron.
Nie wart de tat.
de ghuote de se an ir hat.
lobet se daz ist min rat.

Seghe ich de ghuoten nach mime willen strenghet.
durch daz lez ich de wuonsche vorevaren.
Wuorde min wille mit irme willen menghet.

an eynem bette uns tzuo samende scaren.
Lichte iz also gaat.
daz se des nicht enlaat.
Iz so na.
von ir wart mir eyn leplich ya.
daz vinde ich aber al da. a. a.

I greet you, May, and grant you praise and honor,
my lady comes in all the springtime color
and finery which you have urged upon her;
when snow and ice were here, her clothes were duller.
She's opened up her chest
and donned her very best,
now here is she
as if to say: 'Just look and see,
you men and women, look at me.'
My lady knows I sing of Maytime splendor,
but I would rather listen to her speaking;
her charms are manifold, her heart is tender,
of thousands she's the one whom I've been seeking.
So fair is she alone
beneath the heaven's throne;
there's none as nice,
as kind this side of paradise;
so sing her praise, is my advice.

If she should seem to welcome my advances,
then I may hope to see my love requited,
and should I read my wishes in her glances,
upon a bed we soon would be united.
It easily may be
the lady will agree
on nothing less
and I shall hear a loving 'Yes,'
and then find endless happiness.

Nu nemet war.
manigherhande riche scar.
behort turney ophphenbar.
darnach wil wir tanzen.
Sus hurtzet vort.

in den vroyden hyr und dort.
komet der sorghen uph eyn ort.
bi den wizen swanzen.
traghet hohen muot.
ymmer durch de vrowen guot.
eyner de mich senfte tuot.
de mac mir wol lonen.
Leghe ob ir luost.
wuorphe mich uph ere bruost.
daz da wourde eyn minnen tzuost.
neyn se wil des sconen.

Noch lebe ich so.
daz ich durch se wese vro.
swere ghemuote traghe ich ho.
diz ist doch vil spilde.
Vil reyne vrucht.
nim mich tzuo dir durch din tzucht.
lose mich von sorghen drucht.
du bist mir ghar wilde.
Wer weyz de tzit.
minne manighem toren ghit.
langhe han ich dir ghebit.
lose mich gar snelle.
Dines sinnes louph.
sturtze mich in minnen knoyph.
daz ich mich in eyne hoyph.
uph din hertze velle.

At break of day
the little birds salute the May
with merry songs and bright array
and thanks for happy hours.
The fields are bright
with blossoms: yellow, red, and white,

a wealth of color greets the sight
from leaves and grass and flowers.
The meadow lies
so fair beneath the summer skies,
a feast for men's and women's eyes
of beauties without number.
What May unfolds
the sun with splendor shapes and moulds;
may he be happy now who holds
his loved one here in slumber.

But look and see
how gay the tournament can be
with jousts and splendid pageantry
and afterwards the dances.
Make haste to share
the many pleasures everywhere
and you will find an end to care
in pretty ladies' glances.
A cavalier
should seek the love of ladies here;
there's one, I think, who holds me dear.
If I only knew it!
If she confessed,
I'd throw myself upon her breast
and there'd be jousting then with zest,
but she would never do it.

I act as though
my suit had brought me joy, I know,
and hide with merriment my woe,
but this is only acting.
My dear, say 'Yes,'
receive me now with tenderness
and set me free from my distress;

I find you most distracting.
Who knows this age?
Who knows how love engenders rage?
Long have I waited for my wage;
Oh free me from this fire!
You vacillate
and drive me into such a state
that I might well refuse to wait,
and seize what I desire.

Helphet mir scallen.
hundert tusent vroyden mer.
wen des meyien bluote kan bringhen.
Rosen de vallen.
an mir vrowen roter ler.
da von will ich singhen.
Tuwinct mich de kulde.
al ir wuortzel smaghes ger.
de sint an ir libe ghestrowet.
Worbe ich ir hulde.
so bedrocht ich vroyden mer.
sus de minnighliche mich vrowet.

Leaves fall in showers
down from all the trees around,
limbs are bare and slender.
Look at the flowers
lying withered on the ground
where they bloomed in splendor.
Frost thus has blighted
all the blossoms that were here,
sad am I to lose these treasures.
You are invited,
since the winter is so drear,
now to join me in other pleasures.

Join in my praises
of the charm which far outstrips
joys which May can bring.
Roses she raises
on her lovely cheeks and lips,
and of them I sing.
Though frost may shake me,
from her body comes a scent,
fragrance of blooms and summer breezes.

If she will take me,
I'll lack naught to be content,
she is everything that pleases.

* The conclusion of the *Abgesang* is missing in the manuscript, but since it repeats the *Stollen* melody, a reconstruction of the tune can be supplied.

Harvest brings a rich supply,
man, your wants to satisfy;
many gifts before us lie,
all that feeds and quickens.
Beer and mead and golden wine,
cattle, geese, well-fattened swine,
these delights are yours and mine,
flocks of noisy chickens.
All that grows upon the earth,
man, was given you at birth
and the water's fishes.
Thus we can have a happy life,
for God....

BIBLIOGRAPHY*

Allgemeine Deutsche Biographie (especially Vol. 43, pp. 680-688). Leipzig, 1875-1912.

ANGLÈS, HIGINI, 'Der Rhythmus der monodischen Lyrik des Mittelalters und seine Probleme,' *Kongressbericht*. Internationale Gesellschaft für Musikwissenschaft, Vierter Kongress. Basel, 1949, p. 45.

BARTSCH, KARL, *Deutsche Liederdichter des zwölften bis vierzehnten Jahrhunderts*. Berlin, 1910.

BARTSCH, KARL, *Deutsche Liederdichter des 12. bis 14. Jahrhunderts. Eine Auswahl*. Leipzig, 1864.

BARTSCH, KARL, *Untersuchungen zur Jenaer Liederhandschrift. Palaestra*, Vol. 140. Leipzig, 1923.

CORTE, ANDREA DELLA, *Scelta di musiche per lo studio della storia*. Milano, 1928. Minnesong IX.

DETMAR, *Chronik des Franciscaner Lesemeisters Detmar*, ed. by F.H. Grautoff. Vol. I. Hamburg, 1829.

Die Deutsche Literatur des Mittelalters. Verfasserlexikon. Vols. I-II, ed. Wolfgang Stammler; III-V, ed. Karl Langosch.

DÖLLING, ALBERT, *Die Lieder Wizlaws III. von Rügen, klanglich und musikalisch untersucht*. Diss. Leipzig, 1926. Musical transcription of the complete manuscript.

ETTMÜLLER, LUDWIG, *Wizlaws des Vierten Sprüche und Lieder. Bibliothek der deutschen National-Literatur*, Vol 33. Quedlinburg & Leipzig, 1852.

---

* In the case of those works which contain musical transcriptions of one or more songs, the song or songs is indicated.

FABRICIUS, CARL GUSTAV, *Urkunden zur Geschichte des Fürstenthums Rügen.* Vol. IV. Berlin, 1859-1869.

FOCK, OTTO, *Rügensch-Pommersche Geschichten aus sieben Jahrhunderten.* Leipzig, 1861.

GENNRICH, FRIEDRICH, *Grundriss einer Formenlehre des mittelalterlichen Liedes als Grundlage einer musikalischen Formenlehre des Liedes.* Halle, 1932. Minnesongs IV and XI.

GENNRICH, FRIEDRICH, 'Liedkontrafactur in mittelhochdeutscher und althochdeutscher Zeit,' *Zeitschrift für deutsches Altertum,* LXXXII (1948), 105-141. Minnesong XII.

GENNRICH, FRIEDRICH, *Mittelhochdeutsche Liedkunst. Musikwissenschaftliche Studienbibliothek,* Heft 10. Darmstadt, 1954. Minnesongs III and V.

GENNRICH, FRIEDRICH, *Troubadours, Trouvères, Minnesang und Meistergesang.* Köln, 1960. Minnesongs III, IV, V, and XII.

GENNRICH, FRIEDRICH, 'Zu den Melodien Wizlaws von Rügen,' *Zeitschrift für deutsches Altertum und deutsche Literatur,* LXXX (1943), 86-102.

GÉROLD, THÉODOR, *La musique au moyen âge.* Paris, 1932. Minnesong IV.

GÜLZOW, ERICH, *Des Fürsten Wizlav von Rügen Minnelieder und Sprüche. Pommersches Schriftum,* Vol. I. Greifswald, 1922.

HAGEN, FRIEDRICH H. v. der, *Minnesinger: deutsche Liederdichter des 12., 13. und 14. Jahrhunderts.* 5 vols. Leipzig, 1838-1861.

HOLZ, G., F. SARAN, E. BERNOULLI, *Die Jenaer Liederhandschrift.* 2 vols. Leipzig, 1901. Musical transcription of the complete manuscript.

HUGHES, DOM ANSELM, Ed., *Early Medieval Music up to 1300. New Oxford History of Music,* Vol. II. London, 1954.

JELLINGHAUS, HERMANN, *Geschichte der Mitteldeutschen Literatur.* Berlin & Leipzig, 1925.

KANTZOW, THOMAS, *Thomas Kantzows Chronik von Pommern in Niederdeutscher Mundart,* ed. W. Böhmer. Stettin, 1835.

KIPPENBERG, BURKHARD, *Der Rhythmus im Minnesang.* Munich, 1962.

KNOOP, O., 'Dichtete Fürst Wizlaw III. von Rügen in niederdeutscher Sprache?' *Baltische Studien,* XXXIV (1884), 277-308.

KNOOP, O., 'Fürst Wizlaw III. von Rügen und der Ungelarde,' *Baltische Studien,* XXXIII (1883), 272-288.

KRAUS, CARL V., *Deutsche Liederdichter des 13. Jahrhunderts.* 2 vols. Tübingen, 1952-1958.

KRUSE, HEINRICH, *Witzlaw von Rügen, Trauerspiel in fünf Aufzügen.* Leipzig, 1881.

KUNTZE, FRANZ, *Wizlaw III., der letzte Fürst von Rügen.* Halle, 1893. Minnesongs VI and XII.

LANG, MARGARETE, *Ostdeutscher Minnesang.* Melodies transcribed by Walther Salmen. Lindau and Konstanz, 1958. Minnesongs I and II, Spruch XII.

LILIENCRON, R. V., STADE W., *Lieder und Sprüche aus der letzten Zeit des Minnesangs.* Weimar, 1854. Musical transcriptions of seven songs.

MOHR, WOLFGANG, 'Zur Form des mittelalterlichen deutschen Strophenliedes,' *Der Deutsche Minnesang.* Darmstadt, 1963. 229-255.

MOSER, HANS JOACHIM, *Geschichte der deutschen Musik,* Vol. I. Stuttgart, 1930. Minnesongs V, VII, and IX.

MÜLLER, K. K., *Die Jenaer Liederhandschrift der Universität Jena.* Jena, 1896.

MÜLLER, GÜNTHER, 'Studien zum Formproblem des Minnesangs,' *Deutsche Vierteljahrsschrift für Literaturwissenschaft und Geistesgeschichte,* I (1923), 61-103.

PYL, THEODOR, *Lieder und Sprüche des Fürsten Wizlaw von Rügen.* Greifswald, 1872.

RIEMANN, HUGO, *Die Musik des Mittelalters. Handbuch der Musikgeschichte,* Vol. I, Abt. 2. Leipzig, 1905. Minnesongs IV, VI, IX, and XII.

SEAGRAVE, BARBARA, THOMAS, WESLEY, *The Songs of the Minnesingers.* Urbana, 1966. Minnesongs I, IV, V, VII, VIII, and IX.

SEELMANN, W., '*Wizlaw III., der letzte Fürst von Rügen.* Von Franz Kuntze,' *Anzeiger für Deutsches Altertum und Literatur,* XX (1894), 343-350.

TAYLOR, RONALD J., *Die Melodien der weltlichen Lieder des Mittelalters.* Vol. I, *Darstellungsband;* Vol. II, *Melodienband.* Stuttgart, 1964. Minnesong III.

TAYLOR, RONALD J., 'A Song by Prince Wizlav of Rügen,' *Modern Language Review,* XLVI (1951), 31-37. Minnesong III.

TAYLOR, RONALD J., 'Zur Übertragung der Melodien der Minnesänger,' *Zeitschrift für deutsches Altertum,* LXXXVII (1956), 132-147.

UTHLEB, ERDMUTE, *Zeilentypen und Strophenformen in der Jenaer Liederhandschrift.* Diss. in progress.

VOGEL, OTTO, *Rügen.* Greifswald, 1887. Contains imitations of Wizlaw by Theodor Pyl.

Volksliederbuch für Männerchor. Leipzig, 1906. (Ed. C. F. Peters). Minnesong VI.

Volksliederbuch für gemischten Chor. Leipzig, 1915. (Ed. C. F. Peters). Minnesong IX.

WEHRMANN, MARTIN, *Geschichte der Insel Rügen.* 2 vols. Greifswald, 1923.
WEHRMANN, MARTIN, *Geschichte von Pommern.* 2 vols. Gotha, 1919-1921.
WEHRMANN, MARTIN, 'Jaromar von Rügen als Elektus von Kammin,' *Pommersche Jahrbücher*, XX (1920), 121-139.
WESTRUP, J. A., 'Medieval Song,' *Early Medieval Music up to 1300. New Oxford History of Music*, Vol. II. London, 1954, Minnesong I.

INDEX OF FIRST LINES

A herre ghot we lebe ist mich (*Spruch* IX), 55, *110-111*
De erde ist untslozen (Minnesong VI), 66, 80-81, *127-129*
De voghelin (Minnesong XI), 66, 68, 83, *142-145*
Dem kuninghe nabughodonosor (*Spruch* VII), 54-55, *106-108*
Der herbest kumpt uns riche nuoch (Minnesong XIII), 66, 69-70, 73, 83, *147-148*
Der unghelarte (Minnesong II), 63-64, 74, 78-79, *118-120*
Der walt und angher lyt ghebreyt (Minnesong IX), 66-67, 82, *136-139*
Dise heylighe tzit (*Spruch* XI), 57, *113-114*
Ich partere dich durch mine vrowen (Minnesong I), 62-63, 74, 78, *117-118*
Ich warne dich vil iungher man ghetzarte (*Spruch* XIII), 57-58, *116-117*
Ich wende buwen uph eyne stat (*Spruch* III), 52-53, *102-103*
Ich wil biten in der tzit (*Spruch* VI), 54, *105-106*
Ihc wil singhen (*Spruch* of disputed authorship), 49-51, 74-75, 86-87, *98-99*
List du in der minne dro (Minnesong IV), 65, 71, 73-74, 80, *122-124*
Loybere risen (Minnesong XII), 66, 69, 77, 83, *145-147*
Manich scimphet uph sin eyghen tzil (*Spruch* XII), 57-58, 72, *114-115*
Menschen kint denket daran (*Spruch* I), 50-52, *99-101*
Meyie scone kum io tzuo (Minnesong VIII), 66-67, 82, *134-136*
Mir geschit nicht wen mir scaffen ist (*Spruch* VIII), 55, *109-110*
Nach der senenden claghe muoz ich singhen (Minnesong III), 64-65, 79-80, *120-122*
Nu rate eyn wiser waz diz si (*Spruch* V), 53-54, *104-105*
O maria din sutze vrucht (*Spruch* II), 52, *101-102*
Saghe an du boser man (*Spruch* X), 56-57, 75, *111-113*
Tzuo rome eyn wunderlist ghescach (*Spruch* IV), 53, *103-104*
We ich han gedacht (Minnesong V), 65-66, 71-72, 74, 80-81, *124-127*
Wol dan her meyie ich ghebe uch des de hulde (Minnesong X), 66, 68-69, 82-83, *139-141*
Wol uph ir stolzen helde (Minnesong VII), 66, 71, 74, 81-82, *130-134*

INDEX OF PERSONS

Agnes of Braunschweig-Lüneburg, 1, 4, 5
Agnes, wife of Wizlaw III, 15
Agnes, daughter of Wizlaw III, 31
Albert, Margrave of Brandenburg, 11
Albrecht II, Count of Anhalt, 32
Alexander IV, Pope, 2
Anglès, Higini, 71
Beatrix, daughter of Heinrich of Mecklenburg, 32
Bernhard II, Prince of Anhalt-Bernburg, 5
Bogislaw IV, Duke of Pomerania, 5, 11
Borchert von Osten, 25
Burkhart von Hohenfels, 60
Christoph, King of Denmark, 30
Curtius, Marcus, 53, 103-104
Daniel (Old Testament prophet), 54
Detmar, 7, 9, 21, 27
Dietrich, Margrave of Meissen, 47
Erich Menved, King of Denmark, 13-16, 18-19, 21-22, 24-26, 28-30, 33
Erich, Duke of Saxony, 22, 27, 28, 31
Erich I, Duke of Schleswig, 3, 5
Ettmüller, Ludwig, 51, 88
Euphemia, wife of Jaromar II, 5
Euphemia, sister of Wizlaw III, 5, 11, 12
Eve, 52
Folz, Hans, 64
Frauenlob (Heinrich von Meissen), 7-9, 20, 52
Friedrich the Serious, Landgrave of Thuringia, 86
Friedrich von Hausen, 46
Friedrich von Sonnenburg, 57, 87
Gabriel, 52
Gennrich, Friedrich, 64
Gerhart of Holstein, 56

Gerhard, Count of Plön, 18
Glareanus, 74
Godeke von Güstrow, 23
Goldener, Der, 7-8
Gottfried von Neifen, 60
Hagen, Friedrich von der, 87-88
Hakon V, King of Norway, 5, 11, 13, 30
Helena, sister of Wizlaw III, 6-7
Heinrich VI, Emperor of Germany, 46
Heinrich VIII, Emperor of Germany, 24
Heinrich, Prince of Mecklenburg, 18-19, 21-22, 27-28, 32-33
Heinrich von Morungen, 44, 70
Heinrich von Osten, 25
Heinrich I, Prince of Werle, 10, 51
Hermann the Monk of Salzburg, 69
Hermann, Count of Thuringia, 47
Jaromar I, Prince of Rügen, 2, 4
Jaromar II, Prince of Rügen, 2-3, 5
Jaromar, brother of Wizlaw II, 6
Jaromar, brother of Wizlaw III, 4, 6, 7
Jaromar, son of Wizlaw III, 31-32
Jesus, 52, 55, 105
Johann von Güstrow, 23
Johann, Prince of Mecklenburg, 5, 7
Johannes of Kamp, 31
Kantzow, Thomas, 2
Kelin, Master, 54
Knoop, O., 49, 53
Lang, Margarete, 78
Livy, Titus, 53
Margarete, daughter of Margrave Albert of Brandenburg, 11
Margarete, wife of Erich I of Schleswig, 5
Margarete, sister of Wizlaw III, 5, 30
Margarete, wife of Wizlaw III, 14, 62
Marner, Der, 54-55
Mary, mother of Jesus, 35, 52, 55, 101-102
Mestwin II, Prince of East Pomerania, 10
Nebuchadnezzar, 54, 106, 108
Neidhart von Reuenthal, 37, 60, 70, 86
Nietzsche, Friedrich, 59
Nikolaus the Child, Prince of Mecklenburg-Rostock, 11
Nikolaus II, Prince of Parchim, 10

Otto the Long, Margrave of Brandenburg, 8
Otto IV, Margrave of Brandenburg, 63
Petrus, Master, 31
Pyl, Theodor, 51
Reinmar von Zweter, 55-56
Rudolf, Duke of Saxony, 29
Rumsland, 54-55
Sambor, brother of Wizlaw III, 4, 6, 10-12
Sophie, sister of Wizlaw III, 5
Steinmar von Klingenau, 69
Ulrich, Count of Lindow, 15
Ulrich von Winterstetten, 60
Ungelarde, Magister, 5, 51, 63-4, 118-120
Uthleb, Erdmute, 87
Waldemar I, Margrave of Brandenburg, 19, 22, 24, 26, 28-30, 32
Waldemar I, King of Denmark, 1
Walther von der Vogelweide, 37, 46, 51, 70, 86
Wartislaw IV, Duke of Pomerania, 24-25, 28, 30-32
Wenzel I, King of Bohemia, 64
Wizlaw II, 1, 3-4, 6-7, 9-13, 15, 51 52, 66
Wladislaw, Duke of Poland, 26
Wolfram von Eschenbach, 35

www.ingramcontent.com/pod-product-compliance
Lightning Source LLC
Chambersburg PA
CBHW031315150426
43191CB00005B/238